WHAT WE DO FOR LOVE

CATS IN THE FAMILY

What We Do for Love: Cats in the Family
Copyright © 2018 by Linda Patterson
All rights reserved.

Trade: 978-0-9996931-4-8
eBook: 978-0-9996931-5-5

Library of Congress Control Number 2018962184

Biography and Autobiography: Personal Memoir

Other than brief excerpts to be used in reviews, no portion of this book may be reproduced in any medium or format without permission from the author. Contact the publisher at the address given below with permission requests.

Author's Note: The names of family members and cats in this book are real. The names of veterinarians, behaviorists and other people have been changed.

Cover artwork by Linda Patterson
Back cover photograph by Linda Patterson

Book Design by Frogtown Bookmaker
frogtownbookmaker.com

Published by Lystra Books & Literary Services, LLC
391 Lystra Estates Drive, Chapel Hill, NC 27517
919-968-7877

lystrabooks@gmail.com
lystrabooks.com

Printed in the United States of America

LYSTRA BOOKS
& Literary Services

Readers' Praise for
What We Do for Love: Cats in the Family

In this poignant and entertaining collection, Patterson deftly explores her relationships with the many cats she has owned and what they have taught her. From being a little girl, whose stoical parents try to abolish all traces of and feelings for her beloved kitty, Boots, Patterson grows into a woman who learns that our feline friends can untidy our carefully curated lives and swell our hearts. Cats, it turns out, can even show us how we want to die.

- Carol Henderson, author of
Farther Along: The Writing Journey of Thirteen Bereaved Mothers

If you have ever had a cat in your life, you'll love these stories! Beautifully written, sad and funny wonderful stories with life lessons revolving around and involving cats. A wonderful read, every word!

- Ruth Moose, professor emerita of creative writing, UNC-Chapel Hill

Cats take center stage in this enjoyable read about life, love, and loss.

- Holly Weston, DVM,
Jordan Lake Animal Hospital

I might not have expected someone with a history of cat allergies to choose a life shared with cats, but that's what Linda Patterson does, and best of all, welcomes us on the journey through her memoir: *What we Do for Love: Cats in the Family*. Her book is absorbing: real, sometimes fall-down funny—I've shared my life with a fair number of cats, but it's never occurred to me to try to share a shower with one—sometimes deeply sad, as cats and humans both travel through inescapable chapters of the life experience. The best thing I can recommend is to read it! You'll be glad you did.

- Joyce Allen, author of *The Threads Trilogy*

This book is dedicated to my late husband, John Watts, and my children, Henry and Grace Watterson.

WHAT WE DO FOR LOVE

CATS IN THE FAMILY

Linda Patterson

LYSTRA BOOKS
& Literary Services
Chapel Hill, NC

THE FORMATIVE YEARS

No More Cats!

It was a cold spring Saturday. I was barely four years old and followed my father around while he did yard work. I watched as he raked away the soggy leaves and sticks that clumped together after the snow melted, his metal rake scratching the raw dirt. He stopped to remove logs stacked across a basement window well so he could clean out the leaves underneath. Suddenly he stopped.

"Don't come over here, Linda," he called over his shoulder. He turned quickly to block my view, but I saw a flash of black and white fur on his shovel.

"Daddy! Is that Boots?"

He didn't reply, but I knew he had found Boots' body. My cat had disappeared in the winter. I ran crying into the house to find my mother. I wept into her smooth, cotton dress as she patted my back.

♦ ♦ ♦

My adult cousin Beverly brought me the black and white kitten the summer before. Beverly was an independent, single woman who spoke her mind. She had a wry sense of humor and loved to tell old family stories that made my father cringe. Adults referred to Beverly as a character, but she had a soft heart and was a devoted animal lover.

As a small child I had always possessed stuffed cats made from rabbit fur. On a previous visit, Beverly noticed my devotion to these pretend pets and asked my parents, out of my earshot, if she could get me a kitten.

"What's its name?" I asked when she presented the kitten.

"Twenty-mile Cat," Beverly said, "because that's how far I drove to pick it up."

The kitten had a black body and white feet, so my parents and I renamed her Boots after Beverly went home.

On Saturday mornings, my father took me to hardware stores and lumberyards while he bought supplies for his home-maintenance projects. I was shy and hid behind his wide pant legs as he talked to the men at these businesses. I loved being with my father and often endured the whirr and scream of power tools in his woodshop just to be with him. I became familiar with the tools and the smells of sawdust and turpentine, but I preferred arranging doll furniture and playing with stuffed animals. I was thrilled to have a real kitten.

One morning less than a year after Boots arrived, I couldn't find her. "Where is Boots?"

My mother said, "She didn't come in last night. I'm sure she will be back soon."

But she didn't come back. She had taken shelter under the logs in the basement window well and lain there until spring. Had she been sick or hurt, and frozen to death? This was my first encounter with death. My father's silence and attempt to hide Boots' body from me made it clear that death was not to be discussed. No one knew exactly what had happened to Boots.

That summer, my parents, brother and I were on vacation in New Hampshire when my maternal grandmother died. We immediately packed up and drove home to Wilmington, Delaware to get funeral clothing and then traveled another three hours to Nana and Papa's house in Pennsylvania. My mother sat motionless in the car and my father drove in silence. As soon as we entered my grandparents' home, my mother sat down at the kitchen table and wept. I had never seen her cry. My aunt hustled me out of the room and ushered me into the living room where my grandfather sat silently and listened to a scratchy recording of "Old soldiers never die, they just fade away."

The next day, the family went to the funeral, but left me in the care of my mother's childhood friend, Delilah, a stranger to me. I spent a bewildering, boring day trying to play with Delilah's children and waiting for my parents to pick me up.

After Boots' death, a succession of three more cats joined our household: Smokey, a tiny kitten with mottled dark gray fur; Maverick, a jet-black beauty; and a gray and white kitten whose name I cannot remember. My most enduring memory of these kittens is my mother's endless patience cleaning up the messes they left discreetly in the corners of the carpeted family room. The cats were mine, but my mother always assumed responsibility for their care.

Each of these cats vanished after a short time. I peppered my parents with questions and cried as I waited for the latest one to return. My parents always murmured something about getting hit by a car or running away. I couldn't imagine why our cats would run away from home. What was not to like? Maybe they didn't like our dog, Paddy, or being treated like toys as I dressed them in doll clothes and spanked them. I didn't know then that there were even more dangers for cats outdoors in addition to being hit by a car—lapping up something poisonous such as antifreeze or being eaten by a predator, to name two.

My grandfather, Papa, died when I was ten and old enough to attend his funeral. His casket was open according to his new wife's wishes. My mother and her sisters were outraged: They thought open caskets were barbaric. There were flowers, but no gladiolas because Papa disliked them and called them jungle flowers. My grandfather and his brother died within a day of each other so the next day we went to the reception after my great uncle's funeral. I didn't know these relatives, but could pick them out because Papa's side of the family was short. I was tall like my father. My mother dressed me in a dark blue print dress with a sleeveless coat and a hat that made me feel even taller. Appearances were important to her and she enjoyed dressing me in the latest fashion. I went along with it although at times I felt silly. My friends didn't dress like this.

We acquired another cat that year: Maggie, a light gray tabby. She survived longer than any of my previous four cats. My mother seemed to genuinely like Maggie and talked to her as if she were a member of the family.

One Saturday afternoon while I was in the yard I heard the screech of tires. I ran to see what had happened and found Maggie bloody and writhing in the gutter. I didn't know what to do and ran for my father. He managed to get Maggie into a cardboard box and we drove her to the vet. My parents and I sat silently on the red vinyl chairs in the waiting room while Dr. Rosenthal checked her out and cleaned her up.

"Nothing wrong that won't heal," Dr. Rosenthal told my father. "But she needs to be immobilized." We brought her home and my father built a small wooden cage to keep Maggie still until her limbs mended. My mother tucked a stuffed animal and a ticking clock next to Maggie and took charge of nursing her back to health. I was glad my parents knew what to do.

Maggie survived her accident, but like my other cats, she too disappeared within the year. We waited for her to return, but after a few months I faced the fact that I had lost Maggie. I wailed. We were all sad. Maggie had been around long enough for my parents to become attached to her.

My father never said much when my cats disappeared, but my mother always came up with their stock explanations, "Maybe she ran away. Or got hit by a car." Neither parent was comfortable with my displays of grief. My childhood was a roller coaster of emotions: joy when I acquired a cat, and despair when I lost it. After Maggie, my father could not bear to see me cry again over a pet. He put his foot down, declaring, "No more cats."

Staying Power

When I was twelve, my friend Mary and I went to the annual Wilmington Flower Market, a major charity event in Delaware. Mary's father dropped us off and we felt grown up to be on our own for the day. Smells of popcorn and cotton candy drifted through the air as we wandered past kiddie rides and concession stands. A band played in the background as we visited tents filled with crafts, homemade candy and flats of flowers and vegetables for sale.

We skipped most of the tents promoting community organizations until we came to one sponsored by a local animal shelter. We were attracted by a large circular cage holding tiny kittens, all piled on top of each other. A gray tabby crawled over two sleeping orange tabbies as a tiny black cat huddled against the wire cage. There were a couple of calicos, a white one and gray kittens in various stages of repose. But the one that caught my eye had tan fur, different from any cat I had ever seen. He drew my sympathy because he lay on the bottom of the pile, being stepped on by the other kittens.

"So cute! I want another cat," I exclaimed. Mary and I found a pay phone and I called my parents. My mother answered.

"Can I please have another cat?" I asked. "There are these adorable kittens here and we haven't had a cat for so long. Please? I will pay for it and take care of it. Please, can I get one?"

My mother called my father to the phone. "Pat! Linnie is on the phone and she wants to bring a kitten home." I heard him groan. I held my breath while they talked. They relented and said I could bring home a kitten. They were busy getting ready to host a dinner party that evening. Maybe the distraction worked in my favor.

Mary and I hurried back to the tent with the kittens. Pointing toward the bottom of the kitten cage, I said to the woman in charge, "I want the little tan one on the bottom."

"You need an adult's permission," she said.

My mouth dropped open and I said, "But I just called my parents and they said it's OK."

She busied herself at the desk. "I'm sorry, an adult needs to be here to give you permission."

"No, really, my parents said it's OK," I insisted.

"I'm sorry. You need an adult." She stood firm.

My throat tightened and I wiped the tears from my eyes before they spilled down my cheeks.

"That's not fair," Mary whispered as we turned away. She spotted a friend of her father's strolling by. She waved and said. "Hi, Mr. Rand."

"Oh, hi, Mary. How are you?" he asked.

"I'm fine, but Linda wants to get a kitten, and her parents said she could, but the lady said she has to have an adult with her," Mary said.

"That's too bad."

"She only needs an adult to say she can. Could you do that?"

"Oh ... ah, yes, I guess I could."

The three of us went back into the tent and Mr. Rand told the woman, "Linda can have a kitten."

It was a shaky premise to have a man who had never seen me before take responsibility for a cat he would never see again, but I got my kitten.

The tiny kitten curled up in the multicolored straw hat I had purchased at the event. I carried him in the hat all day until Mary's father came to drive us home.

I stood in the doorway of our kitchen with my new kitten. I could see that my mother was busy. Pots were boiling on the stove and the smell of a roast wafted from the wall oven as she chopped vegetables on the butcher-block counter. She was in full swing preparing for her dinner guests but stopped and came over to see the kitten still sleeping in the hat.

"He's so little!" she said. "He must be hungry." She turned down the stove and went upstairs to find a baby-doll bottle hidden away with my outgrown toys. Back in the kitchen, she pushed the pots around on the stove to find a spot to warm some milk. After she checked the milk's temperature by placing a drop on her wrist, she filled the bottle. I held the tiny bottle to the kitten's mouth and he ate hungrily as my mother watched. Once he had eaten, she went back to preparing for her party and I carried my kitten upstairs to my room.

All evening, I heard the murmur of party guests and the tinkling of dinnerware, punctuated by my mother's explosive laugh. My parents entertained frequently, usually hosting their bridge clubs. On those nights my mother kept me busy wrapping the prizes she would award. Tonight was not a bridge night, so I was free to sit on my bed and play with my kitten. I mulled over names and decided on Sandy because of his solid tan color.

When I announced his name the next morning, my mother sighed and said, "That's so trite. Let's think of something more interesting. How about Henry?"

As usual, my mother prevailed and we named him Henry. This turned out to be a fine, distinctive name except for the fact that the man at the other end of our street was named Henry. Months after we got my Henry, he told my mother that every time he heard her call, "Henry," he wanted to shout back, "What do you want?"

Henry the cat had distinguishing characteristics besides his tan color and name. He had six toes on each of his front paws, giving him the appearance of wearing mittens. Since he was my sixth cat, had six toes and went on to survive longer than any of my other cats, I decided that six was my lucky number.

We suspected that Henry had been taken from his mother when he was too young. He sucked the strands of a fuzzy red cotton rug until they stood up on end. My mother suggested he was simulating nursing. He slept with this rug every night. When we went on vacation and boarded him at the animal hospital, we made sure the rug went with him.

I had promised to take care of my new cat. My mother frequently asked me to feed Henry at dinnertime, but I always found an excuse: "I need to practice the piano," or "My playing with him feeds his soul." I am sure she rolled her eyes in exasperation. She never forced the issue and fed him herself.

My idea of playing with Henry was one-sided. I twirled a long reed in a circle and he chased it until he was panting. Or I used him as a science experiment. At this time, we lived in a home with five-foot-deep basement window wells. I had heard that if you drop a cat from a height, it can right itself before hitting the ground. One of these window wells seemed the perfect place to test this theory. As I held Henry upside down over the window well, he flailed and twisted trying to right himself. In his panic, his claw caught my right eyelid and ripped it. I was embarrassed when I told my parents how my eyelid had been torn and did not garner much sympathy.

Henry had lived with us for four years by the time I entered high school. I started to sneeze loud, furniture-shaking exhalations and my nose ran at inconvenient times. I had developed asthma. Testing revealed allergies to dust, mold, dogs and cats. I started a course of shots that I administered to myself by piercing the skin of my thigh with a needle and slowly pushing the plunger of the syringe to discharge the serum into my flesh. Having this control appealed to me more than having someone else give me the shot. I continued these injections through college but stopped when new rules required me to get them in a doctor's office.

Henry stayed at home when I went to college. Going away to study art provided respite from cat fur. Classes, art studio time and my social life kept me busy. My parents took care of Henry while I attended college in Ohio, worked in New York City and went to graduate school in Rochester, N.Y.

While in graduate school, I lived in a house with a roommate who had a cat named Sister. The cat had black and white markings resembling a nun's habit. Sister had a fetish for two tiny Japanese dolls I had on display in my room. After a while I noticed that their faces were scuffed. Sister would go into my room when I was at school and take the dolls downstairs in her mouth. My roommate repeatedly found them in the living room and put them back upstairs. This curious behavior and the dirty footprints Sister left on the toilet seat did not endear her to me. Cats had lost their charm. Only my attachment to Henry remained.

THE BOSTON YEARS

Making the Transition

After graduate school I moved to Boston to start my career as a graphic designer. One day I received a letter from my mother. She had hand-colored a black border around the page. I didn't understand the significance of this when I first opened the letter. As I read, I realized my parents had euthanized Henry. He was fourteen and had lost control of his bodily functions. I am sure they agonized over this decision, but weeks had gone by before they notified me of his death.

My shock and sadness turned into fury. When did he start having problems? Why hadn't they called me with the news? Why send a letter that took days to reach me? Even though I had left Henry in their care, he still belonged to me, my only cat that had survived more than a year or two. I racked my brain to understand their delay. My parents were kind people, but they didn't like conflict or emotional displays. Were they afraid of my anger or grief? Calling to tell me about Henry's death would not have been easy. I already knew they didn't talk about death.

I called them to let them know how hurt and angry I felt, but they only said, "He was old and losing control. He wasn't happy. It was cruel to keep him alive."

I never got a satisfactory explanation of why they didn't let me know about his death sooner. I could sympathize with their dilemma, but my hurt at not being notified in a timely manner remained. I poured my grief into creating a woodblock print of a lifeless cat, its black shape lying flat along the bottom edge of the rice paper. It wasn't much to look at, but it captured how I felt. Henry was gone and it seemed as if his death had closed the chapter on cats.

I was keenly aware of having moved away from my childhood. I missed the social structure of a school that surrounded me with friends. I created another woodblock print of myself as a young child in a 1950s dress. I am in the foreground, printed in black and white, but my back is toward the viewer as I look toward the horizon at a brightly colored child's drawing of a house and a cat. The child in me was looking wistfully at the past.

♦   ♦   ♦

When I was twenty-seven, I met John Watts, a lanky, red-haired man, who had also owned a cat named Henry when he was a child. John was smart and had a great sense of humor. When we married, we had a tacit understanding that we would never get a cat because of my allergies.

Before our first child was born, we went through lists and lists of baby names. We knew we were having a boy and we considered Owen, Forrest, Bennett, Mark, Peter, Benjamin and Gaird (my grandfather's name). In the end, we agreed on Henry. We weren't naming our child after our cats, but we both liked the name. For his surname we combined the syllables of our last names, Watts and Patterson, to make a new last name, Watterson.

When our son attended middle school, the students were asked to write a story about the origin of their first or last names. "There is nothing special about my names," Henry told the teacher. We were amazed that he failed to recognize the significance of his names: His first name harkened back to our childhood cats, and his last name was a combination of our last names. He certainly knew the stories, but perhaps he didn't like having an unconventional last name or thinking he was named after cats.

As parents and homeowners, we ran a tight ship and were fastidious housekeepers. We cleaned the house every week and kept toys out of sight. We had a place for everything and kept everything in its place. Pets were out of the question because I wouldn't have suffered pet hair collecting in the corners of my house or on my upholstered furniture. In those years, I was happy to be away from cats: They made me sneeze and they shed.

Major Losses

When our son Henry was four, we adopted one-year-old Grace from Korea. Henry had been an easy child, precocious and verbal. We put him in his crib with a stack of books and he would leaf through them and go to sleep. Grace was a different story. She was active and always looking for interaction. Grace loved animals and wanted to cuddle them. Henry was more interested in chasing birds to get a reaction. Neither child ever said, "Why can't we get a dog?" or "I want a cat." It seemed to be a non-issue, much to my relief.

Henry was twelve and Grace was nine when my mother died unexpectedly. Mom was at home recovering from colon cancer surgery when she felt so ill she asked to go back to the hospital. I flew to Delaware a few days before she passed away. My father and brother had met with doctors, but they wanted to believe she was going to get better. If they absorbed her dire condition, they didn't share it with me. My first clue was seeing the "Do Not Resuscitate" sign on her door.

"Why is there a DNR sign on my mother's door?" I asked a nurse at the nursing station.

"Because she's dying," she said.

Communication in my family was often missing or off-target. When I got to the hospital, even before I saw my mother, my brother grabbed my arm and said, "Don't tell Mother that Kathy and I are separated." It was the first I had heard of this.

No one in the family nor her doctor had planned to tell my mother about her condition, either. When she asked me if she was going to have another surgery, I dodged the question by saying she had to get stronger first. I remember hearing her ask my father, "What will become of me?" He was silent. There were no family deathbed chats, no goodbyes, no "I love yous."

My father and I tried to sleep in my mother's room the night before she died despite her labored breathing. My brother was out of town. At around 6 a.m., my father asked me to take him home to go to bed. I was horrified. It was clear my mother was near death and I wanted to be there when she passed away. I was curious about the dying process. Would we see her soul rise above her body?

I drove my dad home and we both slept until 10 a.m., when I was awakened by a call from the hospital. The nurse said, "Mrs. Patterson's condition has changed. You should come to the hospital right away."

"You mean she has died?" I said.

"I'm telling you her condition has changed. That's all I can say." Once again no one was being straightforward about death.

My father and I sat with my mother's body for a few minutes, and then he left the room. I stayed a little longer and complimented the hospice worker on how she had arranged my mother's hair. My father and I retreated to the hospital cafeteria in stunned silence. Over and over we said, "I can't believe it."

When we returned home my father asked me to clean out my mother's personal clothing and jewelry right away. That evening he had his picture taken for the church directory. I expressed surprise, but he said he wanted to keep his appointment. He was carrying on in the face of sadness, probably because he didn't know what else to do.

A year before my mother died, she told me on the phone, "You know what I want for my funeral? I want Henry to sing 'The Lord's Prayer' and the congregation to sing 'A Mighty Fortress is Our God.'"

I was stunned, but wrote this down. After she died, I realized what a wonderful gift it was to have a memorial plan. Twelve-year-old Henry was a quick study and I taught him Malotte's "The Lord's Prayer" as I drove him to school each morning the week before the memorial service. The congregation sang the hymn she wanted and Henry sang "The Lord's Prayer" and a song in German. I delivered a eulogy. Per her wishes, we had her cremated and the ashes buried in the church memorial garden.

I couldn't escape the shock of losing my mother. She and I had had a contentious relationship so there was some relief from her critical tongue, but from time to time, the momentousness of my loss swept over me. I would look up at John and the children at the dinner table and say, "I can't believe my mother is dead." John was always supportive and replied sympathetically, "Yes, it is very sad." Henry and Grace just stared at me in bewilderment.

Two years later when my father lay dying, I was no better at talking about death than he had been. We both knew what was happening as he became weaker and weaker, but neither he nor I approached the subject. I resembled my father in looks and temperament. He was my touchstone. I knew I would cry if I admitted I was losing him. Daddy didn't like to see me cry.

I didn't have the courage to talk to him about his impending death. I consoled myself by thinking I was following his lead by not bringing it up. The only time we came close to the subject was when I reassured him that I would keep his father's sheepskin diploma safe. Ours was a family culture of stoicism and unvoiced love.

My father had been a longtime member of the church choir so I asked the choir to sing at his service. Once again, I delivered the eulogy. He, too, was cremated and his ashes buried in the church garden.

I never shed a tear when my mother died, but I closed my eyes as the tears streamed down my face when my father's service ended.

With both of my parents gone, I experienced an interior emptiness and my belief in God began to fade. I longed for all that had been lost and sought comfort in the memories of my childhood. One of those treasures was my love of cats. Fantasies of having a cat began to weave in and out of my thoughts. I kept this to myself so as not raise false hopes in my husband and children, but started to test my idea.

My friend Pat had a little tabby cat named Hillary. One day as we sat in her backyard, I picked up Hillary and sniffed her fur. I didn't sneeze or cough and my nose didn't run. This was encouraging. Again and again when opportunity presented itself, I pressed my nose into the fur of cats without consequence. Later, my allergist viewed my methodology with skepticism, but I had buried my nose in enough cat fur to convince myself that it was safe to bring a cat into our home.

Steve, the Wonder Cat

"I want to get a cat," I announced one evening. John raised his eyebrows and my children expressed cautious surprise. "I am serious. I have been sniffing cat fur and haven't had a reaction so I think we can get a cat."

I had thought this through carefully because I knew Grace would be particularly upset if I didn't live up to this promise. We agreed to find a cat when we returned from a much-needed vacation in Mexico. As we drove home from the airport we brainstormed cat names.

"How about Esperanza? It's my favorite name," John said.

"What would you call the cat? Espy? Ranza?" I dismissed his suggestion. "How about Leo?" I asked. Silence. "Harley? Toby? Jet? Gretchen? Spot? Tigger?" I added.

"How about something a little classier, like Steve?" John asked.

That elicited laughter from all of us. I wrote that one down on the list.

Our children wanted a kitten, so I called animal shelters asking if they had young cats. Only one did: two gray tabby kittens. Gray tabbies seemed so common. I wanted more options so I expanded my search and called shelters farther away. It was late August and again and again, I was told, "Sorry, spring is kitten season."

With limited options, we piled into the car on a Saturday and drove into Boston to look at the gray tabbies.

At the shelter, John and I tried to convince Henry and Grace to consider an older cat because so many needed homes. John and I looked at all the cats in the back room. He was enthralled by the biggest cat he had ever seen—two feet high, by his telling—while I had my eye on a solid gray female named Nala. Our teenaged son, sporting age-appropriate detachment, spent most of his time in the lobby looking at the fattest cat any of us had ever seen.

Grace played with the two kittens. They held no charm for me. They were gawky with giant ears. Grace bonded with the one that ran into the wall when she teased him with a string.

The name posted above his cage was Bob. I liked the other one because his tawny fur was an unusual color, but I was overruled. I lifted Bob onto the counter to complete the paperwork for his adoption. When asked for his name, I wrote Steve.

Despite the reservations John and I had had about getting a kitten, all of us fell in love with Steve. It is difficult not to be won over by a baby animal. We all wanted to hold Steve, play with Steve and be involved with Steve. With this positive ego reinforcement, he grew into a confident, highly social cat. He was smart, engaging and fearless. He sat on the kitchen counter and watched as we washed dishes; he sat on the workbench in the basement and watched John repair appliances; and he sat on the cold tile in the bathroom and watched us bathe or take showers.

Steve mastered the cabinets and doors in our home. He could push open the lazy Susan cupboard door until it swung around to reveal his cat food. The doors in our house had wrought iron latches instead of doorknobs, so he learned to reach up and pull down the thumb latch to release the bolt. He was particularly fond of checking on people in the bathroom, family and visitors alike. When we had friends from Mexico staying with us, Steve rattled the thumb latch while Coquina sat in the bathroom. She thought her husband was fooling around and she shouted in Spanish, "Bernardo, stop it." The rattling continued until Steve undid the latch, walked in and surprised her.

When Steve was young, I allowed him to go outside on his own. We lived in a quiet suburb with a grassy yard edged with mature bushes. There was a lot for a cat to explore. Steve was confident, and I didn't doubt his ability to take care of himself or find his way back to the house. I worked from home at the time and let him out and brought him in as I saw fit.

One day the doorbell rang. My postal carrier stood there holding Steve. "I'm sure you don't want this guy outside," he said. I thanked him, brought Steve in and soon let him out the back door again.

John called Steve "the inspector general" because he always checked his territory, everything and everybody in it. He monitored our house and neighborhood, chasing cats and dogs out of our yard. He didn't have animal friends, but people found him charismatic.

A year after finishing our neighbor's home addition, the builder asked her, "How's Steve?" Our neighbor didn't know whom he was talking about. "You know, Steve, the cat who always came around while we were working," he said. The builder used to back up his truck to the front door and leave the doors open for easy access. Steve would cross the street, jump in, sniff the tools, walk the length of the truck and enter the house.

Steve was a competent predator, too. Once we came home to find a trail of feathers in the house and blood on the basement walls. I imagined Steve had carried a bird through the cat door in the basement, and then chased it as it flew through the house trying to escape his teeth and claws. When he caught it, he took it outside again. A few days later we found a bird's body on our front patio.

Steve enjoyed spending time with Grace, exploring the jumble of toys and clothes on the floor in her room. She liked to dress him up in doll clothes and sometimes made him custom cat clothing. With a bonnet tied under his chin, he sat contently in her doll stroller as she wheeled him around the house.

Steve was the king of his castle. He had the freedom to come and go, but his life was about to change.

One Was Not Enough

We all adored Steve and competed for his attention. I pictured each of us holding one of his legs and pulling in opposite directions. I entertained the idea of getting a second cat to take the pressure off Steve. My allergy symptoms had not returned in the six months Steve had lived with us so adding another young cat to our household seemed reasonable. In the back of my mind I knew I was taking a chance.

It was February. Again shelters told me they wouldn't have kittens until spring, but I persevered to find a second feline for us. I scoured pet shelter websites, followed leads from pet fostering networks and told everyone who listened that we wanted to adopt a second cat.

A member of a cat lovers' network called me about a young cat named Cutie. This cat had been promised to a woman who never came to claim her. Cutie had been in a large shelter miles away, but now she was housed with a vet near us. I was busy the evening the call came, so John and twelve-year-old Grace drove over to see her.

"Black with orange dots, one orange tabby leg and one white, four white paws, and an orange triangle patch on her face," was John's description. He and Grace seemed neutral about her, so I visited Cutie the next day. Grace came along for a second look.

We sat in the dimly lit waiting room on vinyl-covered chairs. The pervasive antiseptic smell of the veterinarian's office hung in the air. The vet tech brought out a small cat and placed her on my lap. Although Cutie sat quietly, she shed a tremendous amount of fur on to my dark blue coat. "Why is this cat shedding so much?" I asked the tech.

"Oh, she's just nervous. She'll stop shedding in time," she said. How much time, I wondered. Checking this cat over like a used car, I noticed that she had a round belly.

"Is she pregnant?" I asked.

"No, she's been spayed," the tech said. I remained skeptical. John told me later he had asked the same question.

The excessive shedding, the cat's quiet demeanor and my concern that she was pregnant gave me pause, but I signed the papers.

The tech boxed her up in a cardboard pet carrier and I took her out to the car. Grace balanced the carrier on her lap during the ride home. As I drove, we listened to the cat's plaintive cries, muffled by the box. Eager to make a connection with our new pet, Grace stuck her finger into the box's air hole and the little cat bit it, a harbinger of their future relationship.

We did not have any instructions or experience in introducing a second cat into our household. I carried the box into the house and placed it in the middle of the dining room floor. Steve arrived in an instant. He strode over and sniffed the box. The new cat leapt from the closed box and hid under the first piece of furniture she could find: a small antique walnut bureau with only inches of clearance under its carved front panel. Steve stood guard, ready to meet the newcomer. As the minutes ticked by and the excitement waned, I left Grace to watch the two cats. She, too, eventually lost interest and left the cats maintaining their positions.

After Steve became bored and wandered off, the new cat escaped to a high shelf in the corner cabinet. Hours later when John came home from work, she was still there. John walked over and talked to her softly. She let him pet her and she quickly learned whom she could trust.

This cat was so unusual looking that we renamed her with difficulty. Traditional names, sophisticated names, familiar names, nothing seemed to fit. She was very cute, but we couldn't abide an insipid name like Cutie. The triangular orange patch over one eye gave her panache, so I finally chose the name Cairo for no other reason than it sounded exotic. It is possible John's brass statue of an Egyptian cat in our living room influenced me. Cairo took well to her name, but responded best to the one-syllable version, Cai. And sometimes when John felt particularly affectionate, he called her Cai-Cai.

Cairo was definitely not what we had in mind when we imagined life with a second cat. I expected a second Steve. Grace wanted a cat to cuddle and dress up. John wanted a lap cat as engaging as Steve. Henry liked the new cat because she was quiet and timid. He found Steve to be too assertive, and felt we had gotten Steve to replace him when he went to boarding school.

Cairo was not like Steve in intellect or temperament. She was skittish and perpetually frightened. No one could hold her for more than a couple of seconds because she fought and struggled to be free, a behavior she retained for years. Despite her desperation, Cairo never bit anyone other than the initial nip she gave

Grace. She remained anxious, but her shedding eventually stopped. And, the vet tech was right: She never had kittens. She kept herself safely tucked away, crouched under furniture, where she could keep an eye on all of us.

John had a soft spot for Cairo and assumed the role of her protector. Grace spent years trying to cuddle and hug Cairo to no avail. "Put the cat down," John boomed every time he saw Grace embracing Cairo against her will.

In frustration, Grace started calling Cairo "fatty," but once again, John defended Cairo. "Cairo is not fat," he said, "she has an endomorphic body type."

Although she didn't like being picked up, Cairo craved affection. She often greeted us by rolling on her back as if asking for a tummy rub. She squirmed nervously when we petted her, but she was content to have John comb and brush her.

Cairo released a lot of nervous energy when she played. She became very excited when we brought out the pink feather wand or the fake fur tail on a stick. She grabbed the scratching post with her front paws, turned herself upside down and kicked wildly at the post with her back paws.

After John vacuumed each week, he tossed cat toys around the house so they were readily accessible. If Cairo didn't find the toy she wanted on the floor, she went to the toy basket, nosed through the selection of catnip animals, furry mice, fuzzy creatures and crinkle balls, and lifted one out with her teeth. She particularly liked the toys filled with catnip and licked them until their fur was stiff.

Steve and Cairo coexisted well despite their different temperaments. He was dominant and she was timid, so the hierarchy was clear. She was always aware of him and adjusted her behavior accordingly. She walked along the edges of the room, ready to hide and take refuge under tables or chairs if she perceived a threat.

Cairo may have been timid, but she was no wimp. When she and Steve wrestled, they body-slammed each other onto our hardwood floors. Steve was bigger and more aggressive, but he tended to cry during these encounters, so we always judged Cairo the winner.

We spent a lot of time letting cats in and out. We had no trouble getting them into the house in the evening because we trained them to come home for dinner when we rang a bell. Letting them in and out during the day was more challenging. We decided to install a cat door. John was handy and removed an old basement window, created a new one with the cat door in the middle pane and screwed it into the window frame. Now the cats had the freedom to come and go on their own.

When Steve and Cairo went out through the cat door, they led independent lives. Steve checked his territory while Cairo stalked chipmunks and voles. She often sat patiently waiting for a vole to emerge from its hiding place under the children's playhouse or deep in the garden's pachysandra ground cover. When she caught her prize, she brought it into the house while it was still alive. There, she either dropped it or it wriggled free, so she and Steve chased frightened voles and chipmunks behind furniture and under radiators. John tried to catch the small animals before the cats did. He had a special shoebox reserved for this task. Most of the time the rodent was ushered outside, but there were times when John couldn't find it and the cats lost interest. We probably had a hidden roommate or two for a while.

One morning before leaving for work, John kissed me goodbye as I lay in bed dozing. When I awoke I noticed a strong odor. I went through my morning routine, but when I returned to the bedroom the odor still lingered. Following the smell, I found a dead vole under our bed. I scooped it up, flushed it down the toilet and washed the floor to eradicate the smell. When John came home I said, "I found a dead vole under our bed this morning. It smelled terrible."

He paused and said, "Yeah, I smelled it too but thought you had morning breath."

Cairo did not limit herself to hunting in our yard. She travelled two blocks away to the woods. Either the hunting was better there, or she had chosen a location out of Steve's territory. And she didn't restrict herself to catching small animals. One day she brought home a child's shiny pinwheel in her mouth. We returned the pinwheel to our neighbor and bought Cairo her own, but she never gave it a second look. Was it the thrill of the hunt that motivated her theft?

Outside, Cairo seemed fearless, but in the house she was anxious. We often speculated as to the origin of her anxiety. Maybe she had been feral and not socialized with people. Perhaps she endured trauma as a kitten, or maybe she just had a timid temperament. Whatever the reason, John's gentle nature nurtured Cairo, so she found a secure place in our household. Each evening after dinner they sat together on the couch. Cairo enjoyed the warmth of John's lap as he watched the TV news; he had finally gotten the lap cat he had always wanted.

The Coyote

One Saturday afternoon while Steve and Cairo were outdoors for the day, John and I cleaned the house. As John vacuumed near a window, he spied a flash of gray fur in our backyard. He went to the glass door and saw what looked like a well-fed gray dog under a stand of hemlock trees. He had grown up in the west and recognized the animal as a coyote. He ran outside to the porch. "Hey, get out of here!" he shouted. The coyote just looked at him, so John hurried down the porch stairs yelling and waving his arms. The coyote continued to stand there, sizing him up. Then it looked up into a tree. John followed the coyote's gaze and saw Steve clinging to a branch. "Go! Get out!" he yelled.

Eventually the animal turned and sauntered through our backyard, down the gravel path to the driveway, and through our neighborhood on the sidewalk.

The commotion brought me outside. I saw Steve in the tree at the end of our yard. Out of the corner of my eye I caught Cairo dashing across the next-door neighbor's lawn to the cat door in our basement window. She had hidden under our neighbor's deck, twenty feet from our home. With one cat safe, John made sure Steve headed for the house.

John had run out of the house and the cats had run back in so fast, I didn't know what had happened. "What were you yelling at?" I asked.

"That was a coyote," John said. "He was so brazen. He just stood there and looked at me. I yelled and he still didn't move."

We decided immediately that the cats would now be indoor cats. A week later, our neighbor saw the coyote return to our yard around noon, presumably looking for lunch.

Staying in the house was not easy for our cats; they sat at our back door and cried. They pawed and stared longingly at it. If we wanted to get out the back door we had to step into a tangle of cats and make ourselves as thin as possible to squeeze through the doorway without letting them escape.

The whining and congestion at the back door annoyed us, but we were sympathetic. We brainstormed ways to get the cats outside safely. Maybe we could train them to walk on leashes. We purchased two harnesses and leashes: a blue set for Steve, a red one for Cairo. After the initial awkwardness of figuring out which leg went through what strap to get the harnesses on snugly, we snapped on the leashes and opened the door. Steve and Cairo bolted out and went as far as their leashes allowed. Being tethered to a human was not ideal. Cairo could no longer travel to her hunting ground and the length of the leash barely let Steve sniff or mark foundation plantings in front of neighbors' homes.

Steve eventually learned to navigate down the sidewalk with only a few diversions. Sometimes he wanted to go one way when I wanted to go the other. When that happened, he planted himself on the sidewalk, refused to move forward and backed out of his halter until I stood there with an empty leash. Fortunately, he allowed me catch him so I could put him back in the harness and resume our walk.

When it was time to go home, he often tried to back out of the harness again. I needed to pick him up and heft him back to our house, although he maintained a low, ominous growl. I carried him as far away from my body as I could in case he lashed out. When inside, I worked quickly to undo his harness and leash so I could leave the room. More often than not, he attacked me right inside the door. Such was the nature of arguing with a cat. If he had been a child I would have heard whining and vitriol. Instead of words, Steve communicated with his growls, claws and teeth.

The cats were not the only ones that had to adjust. John made time most days after work to walk each of them for a half hour. He matched his pace to theirs and went where they led. Constantly alert to danger, they proceeded slowly. They walked a few feet and stared. They stopped and lifted their noses to catch a scent on a breeze. They sat with ears erect and listened. Cairo had a remarkable capacity to sit and monitor vole activity for long periods. When John felt awkward following Steve and Cairo into the neighbors' yards, he bought new sixteen-foot leashes so the cats could explore deeper into foundation plantings while he stood on the sidewalk. He had time to absorb the neighborhood as he waited for them to slink in and out of foliage. He saw things he had never noticed before like a dying tree or a weathering paint job. Walking cats became a Zen experience.

Taking the cats out every day was time-consuming for us and not completely satisfying for them. I looked for other solutions. After researching cat enclosures on the web, we tried a freestanding cage on wheels that could be parked near us while we did yard work. As we pulled weeds or raked, the cats cried. Being trapped in the cage outdoors was no substitute for walking around in the natural world. We parked the empty cage in our basement.

More research led us to installing outdoor metal cages on two sides of the house. John had already installed a cat door in the basement window, and now placed another in a first-floor window. Each cat door led to a different cage. The cats visited the side garden from the basement or enjoyed a view of our backyard from the tall cage off our family room. Steve and Cairo particularly liked to sit outside on cool summer mornings before we were awake. The broad-leaved hosta plants tracing the foundation provided shady hiding places when temperatures climbed in the middle of the day.

The cages were anchored in the garden soil so there was no chance the cats could get out. However, small garden creatures could get in. Steve and Cairo pounced on hapless rodents travelling through the cage and brought them into our house. John continued to catch them in his shoebox and return them outdoors. The cats lived indoors now, but they still had plenty of interaction with the natural world.

♦ ♦ ♦

Love of our cats did not overshadow devotion to our children. We spent time with the cats, but much more with Henry and Grace. We happily drove our children to activities, helped with homework, attended weekly track club, soccer and basketball games, created elaborate birthday parties and participated in community theater with them. We worked hard to accommodate everyone's needs.

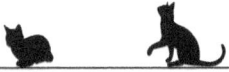

The Maze of Veterinary Care

I fed Cairo and gave her basic care, but she and I never developed much of a relationship. She was a quiet soul and didn't impose herself or demand attention. I took notice the Monday she jumped onto my desk, sat squarely in front of my computer and looked past me. I turned in my swivel chair and followed her gaze to Steve, asleep in a basket nearby. As I thought back, I realized she had been watching Steve for days, even sniffing and licking him, and now she was trying to tell me something.

Steve had always been healthy, with only common feline ailments such as urinary tract infections and occasional vomiting. But over the weekend he hadn't eaten much and had been vomiting more than usual. For a cat on top of everything, he had been lethargic, too.

I made an appointment with our veterinarian, Dr. Petersen, that same day. I watched anxiously as she studied him, and then deftly ran her fingers over his body, prodding his belly. The blood tests she ordered showed high bilirubin.

"This might indicate a liver problem," she said. "Let's have him stay overnight so we can observe him all day tomorrow."

The office was unattended at night, so I opted to bring him back in the morning. After watching him on Tuesday, Dr. Petersen referred us to a well-known animal hospital in Boston for further testing.

John left work early on Wednesday to drive Steve to the hospital. He had a different experience there than in our familiar vet's office. It was as impersonal as any big hospital. John had to fill out paperwork about his ability to pay and leave a down payment. He recounted Steve's symptoms to a staff member, watched as Steve was examined, and then left him at the hospital.

The next day after work, we drove to the hospital to check on Steve as if we were visiting a sick relative. The thirty-year-old building showed its age. There was the familiar smell of dogs, cats and disinfectant. We sat in a dreary waiting room until a staff member ushered us down a dim hall to where Steve crouched in his cage. Our mouths dropped open. Gray wire cages lined the walls of a huge room housing cats and dogs. An examination table stood in the center. Steve's cage was located opposite barking dogs. Yapping, howling and whining reverberated off the walls. Steve huddled in the back corner of his cage but didn't offer resistance when we scooped him out. He sat in John's lap, then pulled himself up and tried to walk. He seemed uncomfortable and ill at ease. We sat awkwardly with him on the floor for a half hour or so and then left with trepidation. We brought him here for help, but his illness, the strange surroundings and barking dogs made Steve even more miserable.

When I went to the hospital to retrieve Steve on Friday evening, I anxiously waited to hear what the medical staff had found. I expected to take notes to accurately report the findings to John. The vet tech handed Steve's carrier to me and said that they had examined him and run tests. The ultrasound showed nothing abnormal.

"But he is not eating and his bilirubin is high." I said. "There must be something wrong."

"No, he is fine," the tech said.

This was shocking. He was not fine. I felt let down by this venerable institution. I carried Steve to the car in his carrier. He was silent. Just as a mother knows her child, I knew my cat. Steve was not well.

On Saturday, Steve still vomited and slept. We took him to Dr. Petersen again that morning. She knew us and trusted our instincts. She drew blood and urine and observed him for another day. Before we took him home for the night, she wanted to cover all the bases and prescribed Denosyl, a nutritional supplement to minimize liver problems; Ursodiol, a bile acid to decrease cholesterol; and three antibiotics, Metronidazole, Ciprofloxacin and Amoxicillin. "A cat's condition can change quickly," she said. "He needs food and water to survive." She handed us a giant syringe to force-feed him and sent us to the main desk to buy specially formulated cat food.

At home, John held him while I tried to wrestle the syringe into Steve's mouth, squeeze the plunger, and force him to swallow the slurry of cat food and water. It was futile. Although sick, he remained strong and squirmed away every time we tried to feed him. We didn't seem able to help him, so we kept him close that night and moved his paraphernalia—cat bed, litter box, food and water bowls—into our bedroom.

Steve had been sick for a week. On Monday, blood test results revealed he was no better. Force-feeding had failed and he wasn't getting food or water. Like us, Dr. Petersen was dismayed by the lack of definitive results from the Boston hospital. She suggested we try a new emergency veterinary facility in Waltham, a nearby suburb. Monday evening, we drove Steve to a very different hospital experience. Everything was clean and modern. The front desk and brightly lit waiting room exuded an appealing sense of quiet and calm. Beyond the front desk lay a series of modern exam rooms and high-tech operating suites. Like the other hospital, pet cages surrounded a central examining table, but cats were on one side of a glass enclosure and dogs were on the other. Steve could rest quietly, undisturbed by barking dogs.

We met with Dr. Jerath, an attractive veterinarian with a reassuring style. Her only flaw was the gray film on her white lab coat. I found this distracting as I tried to listen to her. Despite the facility's sparkling stainless steel, I wondered how clean it was. Time was critical so we left Steve there that evening. Staff would run tests including another ultrasound early the next day. For someone who had refused to leave Steve overnight in our familiar veterinarian's office a week ago, it seemed out of character to now leave him in a strange environment farther from home. I didn't feel I had a choice. Caught in the spiral of acute healthcare, our overriding concern was to help Steve.

The second ultrasound showed that Steve had an enlarged biliary tract. Dr. Jerath asked us to come to the hospital to talk. "I suspect Steve has a blocked bile duct and will need immediate surgery. A tear in his biliary tract could give way any day and fill his abdomen with bile," she said. We gave permission for Steve's surgery to proceed the following morning.

This hospital was accommodating and allowed us to visit Steve the night before his surgery. We sat with him, but he seemed very uncomfortable as he roamed around the exam room. His leg was bandaged stiff to secure an intravenous line but he still jumped from floor to table to chair to floor again. We videotaped him to have a record of this event. He finally settled into a basket and allowed us to pet him. After a while we felt like we were overstaying our welcome because he was cranky, so we reluctantly left him for the night.

We hated to leave him, but his surgery offered us the hope of his renewed health. As we drove home John said, "I can probably work from home while Steve recovers."

"Yeah, I think I can take some vacation time, too," I added. Our son was in college and our daughter away at boarding school. The two of us were the only ones to give Steve twenty-four-hour care. We looked forward to nursing him. We wanted our Steve back in our care to lavish him with love and attention. He was an integral part of our family, a beloved member. We would be there for him.

Wednesday morning, Dr. Jerath kept John apprised by phone. She called when Steve was about to enter surgery and later to say they were able to bypass his blocked bile duct and were in the process of closing. With each call, John relayed the information to me at work. We were elated that the surgery was successful. Then Dr. Jerath called a third time and said, "We are having difficulty waking Steve. He stopped breathing so the tech is manually forcing oxygen into his lungs with an ambulatory bag. She's been going for about twenty minutes."

The fourth and final time Dr. Jerath called, she said, "Steve is gone. After twenty-five minutes, his heart stopped. Our efforts to restart it by massage and injecting chemicals failed. I'm sorry."

John broke down and ended the conversation abruptly. He called me at work again. "Steve is dead," he said. "He stopped breathing after surgery. I'm going home." I was dumbfounded that he was leaving work.

At home, John sat on the couch with Cairo on his lap and watched videos of Steve all afternoon: Steve in his favorite tree, Steve chasing a toy, Steve playing with Cairo, Steve in the yard. He allowed himself to be absorbed by his grief. He confronted it immediately and felt its full force.

I stayed at work and cried briefly at my desk as my boss comforted me. Coworkers came by my desk to console me. I appreciated their sympathy, but as I had been taught, I sublimated my distress. I pulled myself together and went to a meeting. I followed my father's advice to stay busy to cope with life's disappointments whether a teenage heartbreak or a death. My parents expected me to be stoic in adversity. I had learned these lessons well, but losing a pet still made me cry.

When I arrived home, I was surprised that John was still upset. He wanted to talk about our loss. I just wanted it to go away, pretend it never happened. There was nothing we could do, so why dwell on it?

The day after Steve died, a hospital staff member called and asked if we wanted to come and view Steve's body. "What? A chance to see Steve again? Of course!" I thought. We drove over to the hospital soon after work. The carpeted visiting room had comfortable couches, inspirational books and pictures of animals on the wall. A fish tank with a large turtle stood against another wall. After what seemed like a long time, a tech entered and laid Steve's frozen body, wrapped in a blanket, on the couch. He was curled up as if he was sleeping. His gray spotted tabby fur was as beautiful as ever. John stood in front of the couch fighting back tears. We knelt down to be close to Steve. We stroked his soft fur gently. He was cold and creepy to touch, but we tilted him up slightly to peek at the stitches on his shaved belly. His pink tongue lolled from the side of his mouth. Even as we cried, we took clippings of his fur and videotaped and photographed his body. John put his head on the couch next to Steve and I took a photo. Then we switched places and John photographed my crying image. Capturing the images of these last moments with Steve was an important step in our grieving. As long as we had pictures and memories, Steve wasn't completely gone. Those pictures still make me cry today.

All my life I had been told to keep my grief under wraps. The vet's visiting room gave me a safe place to lament our loss and to say goodbye to Steve. The animal hospital gave me permission to mourn openly, something I couldn't give myself. I was glad to have an invitation to grieve.

We shared the videos and photographs with our children. At first Grace didn't realize that Steve was dead in the pictures; he looked like he was sleeping. She was upset by the video of

Steve walking around in the hospital with a bandaged leg. Henry reacted to the pictures of our sad faces by saying, "Why would you take photos of yourselves when you looked so bad?" I was disappointed that he had bought into the family tradition of hiding emotion.

Although I was reserved in public, art was a venue for my feelings. I was a professional artist so recording expressive images, although sad, seemed like an appropriate response to my grief.

"It was art," I told him.

Memories of Steve elevated him to demigod status in John's mind. "Steve was the smartest cat I ever knew," he said. In a conversation years later about losing this beloved cat, I was surprised to hear John's hurt and anger bubble up. "Steve stopped breathing. He didn't even try!"

I was baffled that he could assign such responsibility to an anesthetized cat, but such was the depth of his feeling for Steve.

Memories of Steve endure, maybe because he was our first cat together, or because we raised him from a kitten, or because he was a remarkable creature that was part of our family for five years. Whatever the reason, when I allow myself to travel back in time, my hands feel his fur as I smooth his sleek outer coat and gently push my fingers deep into the soft down underneath.

Now You See Her, Now You Don't

Cairo seemed delighted to be the only cat in the house. We focused our attention on her when we came home from work each day. She stretched out so we could rub her tummy, then wriggled with contentment. Unfortunately, her introverted personality couldn't fill the hole in our lives that losing Steve had left. We missed his intellect, his curiosity and his interest in watching whatever we were doing: washing dishes, doing laundry or repairing things on the workbench. Steve was always around and often the center of attention. John even missed the times that Steve kneaded his chest and carved tiny red marks in his skin. We craved a relationship with a cat as engaging as Steve and found ourselves looking for another cat within weeks of his death. I remembered the old adage to not make any changes for six months after a loss, but I ignored it. I wanted to replace that loss. In one sense we moved on quickly, but we never moved on from our desire to have another Steve.

John drove to Philadelphia one May weekend to pick up Henry from college. Grace and I decided to go cat shopping. Grace loved to shop for anything, but I was looking for a specific type of cat. "I want an all gray cat this time: no stripes, just solid gray. Tabby cats seem so common; cats of a solid color are more unusual," I said. In fact, I wanted a Russian Blue, a breed of cat with a thick gray coat. Grace didn't say anything. She stared at her phone like most sixteen-year-olds.

As we pulled into the parking lot of a large Boston animal shelter, my cell phone rang. A woman returned my call about a Russian Blue she was trying to place in a new home. She talked for forty-five minutes about the virtues of this stray cat. Finally, she said, "There is just one thing. You have to keep him on Prozac, otherwise he urine marks and attacks other cats in the household." That was a deal breaker.

Inside the shelter, Grace and I peered into cages and read the description of each cat. We ricocheted from cage to cage as we oohed and aahed over the cats and tried to respond to each other's calls. "Mom, look at this cute one," or "Oh! A kitten."

"Grace, did you see this one with the unusual markings?" or "Here's a gray cat. Check this one out." I finally found what I wanted: a gray cat. Tiny and hyperactive, she had just weaned a litter of kittens. Although she was available for adoption, she needed to return to be spayed in three weeks.

John and I always made major decisions together, but he was away this weekend. Would he insist on being there when we picked out a new cat? I called him from the cat shelter. "John, Grace and I are looking at cats at the MSPCA and we found a small gray cat. She's really active. I think this is the one we want. Would you be OK if we got her without you being here?" He said he was fine with our decision, so we adopted the small cat. She came home with us and was promptly quarantined in our guest room. The shelter advised us to keep her separated from Cairo for three weeks to protect Cairo from any respiratory infection the new cat might carry from the shelter. On the ride home, we named our new pet Molly. The first day we let Molly roam the house, Cairo kept her distance. Her stint at being an only cat had been brief. I imagine she was distressed to have another cat in the house. John said, "Let's leave Molly and Cairo together tonight to work out their relationship." We went to bed.

The next morning when John went downstairs to feed the cats, he couldn't find Molly. We searched every closet, under every bed and dresser. None of the windows or doors was open. We looked for cracks that she could have squeezed through, put our ears to walls and stood quietly in the basement listening for sounds in the ceiling. We heard nothing. We were puzzled. Indoor cats don't just disappear. We exhausted every indoor possibility and finally considered the cat door in the basement that led to an outdoor cage. There was a gap of fewer than two inches between the cage and the exterior stucco wall of the house. Perhaps this was Molly's egress, but we found no cat hair clinging to the house to suggest she had squeezed through here.

We called the local animal control officer who pointed out that Molly was probably motivated by her hormones to find freedom and another mate since she hadn't been spayed. She must have scrambled through the small space where the cage met the house. She had been out of quarantine for less than eight hours. We were surprised that she had located the cat door in the basement, much less gone through it.

We were left with feelings of disappointment tinged with anger toward Molly. In trying to make sense of her brief sojourn with us, we enjoyed the fantasy that Cairo lured Molly into the outdoor cage, pried open the space between the house and the cage and urged Molly to escape. Cairo would be the only cat in the house again.

We had one picture of Molly. With this photo, we made flyers and posted them around the neighborhood to no avail. Grace remembered Molly as playful and friendly, but she didn't make much of an impression on the rest of us. Every time I walked into the grocery store, I saw Molly's picture on the bulletin board. After a few months, it disappeared just as she had. And, like many of the cats from my childhood, we never saw Molly again.

Not What We Expected

I wanted another gray cat; finding one took longer the second time. John and I visited and revisited animal shelters on the weekends since new pets arrived every week. Now that we had some cat ownership experience, we were prepared to be more discriminating. I read that cats of the same gender were more inclined to fight, so I decided adopting a male would be the best fit for Cairo.

We liked visiting a shelter near our home that housed cats in a small, sunny room with a large window. Toward the end of July, I noticed a solid gray male that I vaguely remembered from a previous visit. He had been moved to a corner cage on the opposite side of the room. Staff moved the animals to different cages each week to give the cats new perspectives and more exposure to visitors. The tag on the cage said this cat had been at the shelter for more than four months. That seemed like a long time to be in a cage.

The gray cat looked at me and I looked at him. I took him out of the cage and called John over. The cat was medium-sized, had a fuzzy gray coat and seemed muscular. After I held him for a bit, he jumped down and started to explore. He walked over to a cage of kittens in the middle of the room, peered in and sniffed. He walked carefully to a corner of the room and nosed around under the rusted industrial sink. He crossed the floor to a wooden bench under the window and jumped up to walk along the cinder block windowsill for a view of the parking lot and the fields beyond. He had lost interest in us, but I was not thwarted; he was gray, male and fit the bill. We paid the fee and signed the paperwork to adopt him, but this shelter's policy required that he be neutered before we took him home.

I wondered why I hadn't seen this cat earlier on Petfinder.com, a site I perused regularly. I looked back at the site and found his picture. He appeared to be a fuzzy gray lump staring stoically into the camera. He had a touch of pathos about him. Even years later whenever we saw that look on his face, we said, "Oh no, he's got his shelter look."

Henry was away at the time, so we installed the new cat in his room for the three-week quarantine. We lined a basket with an old towel to create a bed and put it underneath a desk to give the cat a safe haven. After a day or two, the cat bed reeked of urine, but I left it alone assuming his own scent made our new family member feel at home.

The shelter had named this cat Caesar, but he didn't seem commanding to us. His thick gray fur gave him a soft, endearing look. He seemed quiet and refined. We changed his name to Riley. After he settled in and his personality emerged, we realized how apt his shelter name had been. Although quiet, he quickly became the dominant cat in the household. He kept Cairo in line with a stare or a chase and her timidity ensured his continued high status.

We played with Riley every day. He loved chasing a small furry mouse or leaping high into the air to grab a feather toy, but he also had an aggressive side. Sometimes he jumped on Cairo and bit her neck and sometimes he jumped on us and bit our arms or legs. He attacked us daily, sometimes when we petted him, sometimes when we walked through a doorway and, most perplexing, when we were dishing out cat food. When I came home from work, Riley would greet me by stretching out on the carpet, arching his back and exposing his belly. If I rubbed it, he would bite me. When I continued upstairs, he ran up the stairs to get in front of me, ready to attack again.

We learned to read the warning signs of his attacks: a wild look, dilated pupils and flattened ears. We tried to get out of his way, but he was intent on striking. Sometimes he bit so hard he drew blood. Other times he gently bit me and looked up to see what my response would be. And still other times he attacked quickly, gave a little cry and ran away, his hit-and-run technique.

We tried to manage these daily episodes of aggression by speaking gently to him or not reacting at all. Nothing we did stopped the attacks. One evening, Riley sat and watched me pack for a trip. When I went downstairs to get laundry, Riley jumped up and bit me on the leg twice. I said "no" firmly and Riley cried out. He tried to attack again. This time I pointed at him and said "no" in a loud voice. He gave up, feigned indifference and pretended to groom. A half hour later I called to him. He peeked around the corner and I said, "Play?" I brought out a couple of catnip mice and we played for fifteen minutes.

When hungry, Riley became manic. Many cats wrap themselves around their owner's legs or cry when begging for food, but not Riley. He raced around the house, ran across the fireplace mantel or jumped up on the grandfather clock to get our attention. He reminded me of a hyperactive child. As John stood at the kitchen counter dishing food into Riley's bowl, Riley would jump up and bite his backside. We learned to feed him as soon as he acted hungry for our own safety. We gave him as much food as he wanted as often as he wanted it. Despite years of being fed on demand, he never gained weight.

Riley was clearly intelligent. If I called "out" and he heard the jingle of his leash, he would run to the door. He waited patiently as I adjusted his halter and snapped on the lead. I trained him not to cross the door's threshold until I carried him across. I didn't want him to run outside without me and get lost.

John walked each cat outside on a leash most nights after work. He began taking Riley first, then Cairo. When they returned and John took Cairo out, Riley ran from window to window, crying as he followed Cairo's movements outside. When she came in, he attacked her. John learned to take Cairo out first so that when she returned, Riley was more interested in going out than attacking her.

A year after Riley arrived we had reached our limit with his aggression. I used to fantasize that his previous owner had held open the door one day and said in a loud voice, "Oh, look, Riley, the door is open," in hopes that he would go through it and never return. He was beautiful to look at and had a sensitive soul, but we were not content to live with a cat that attacked us every day.

We spoke to him gently when he was not being aggressive in the hope of encouraging positive behavior. I had read that cats don't respond to punishment; they only respond to positive reinforcement such as treats or petting for behavior we like. We pondered whether he had excess energy and needed a playmate. Cairo hissed at him every time he tried to play with her. Or, did we have a deeper problem and need the help of a behaviorist?

We had called the shelter's cat behavior hot line many times. On our last call, a particularly helpful volunteer recommended the behaviorist who headed their shelter dog program. Although it didn't sound like a perfect fit, we made an appointment. We needed any help we could get.

♦ ♦ ♦

Responding to Riley's behavior was reminiscent of raising Grace. Before she acquired language we were often perplexed by her behavior, but once she learned to talk, she often expressed anger. We were never quite sure how to respond. At times we resorted to yelling, but other times we maintained our cool and spoke calmly. It was not clear what worked. Cats were as baffling as children.

The Behaviorist

Many people have asked why we put up with Riley. Why not return him to the shelter? We didn't like his aggression, but he was playful and intelligent. More importantly, he was a family member. We had sought a therapist's help for our family when our children were young, so we decided to try a pet behaviorist for Riley. We had high hopes that this woman would solve our problems.

The behaviorist mailed us a six-page form entitled, "Feline Behavioral History." John filled out the sections on our household, pet care and the cats' litter box habits, and left the section called "The Problem" for me. I listed Riley's attacks: waiting at the top of the stairs before jumping up to bite and scratch my arm, and biting John's ankle and bottom while waiting to be fed. He was also aggressive with Cairo. As instructed, we faxed this back before our appointment.

The behaviorist's office was housed in the Boston branch of the shelter where we had adopted Riley. John and I sat awkwardly on hard plastic chairs in the drafty hall that doubled as a waiting room. Riley lay in his carrier at our feet. A door burst open and an intense, middle-aged woman swept through, barely motioning for us to follow as she climbed the stairs, all the while talking with an entourage of staffers. Finally, we sat alone with her in the relative quiet of her office, a basic room with painted cinder block walls.

We watched her sift through stacks of papers on her desk, framed by a filmy window behind her. She said she hadn't received the questionnaire we had faxed. And, she muttered that she didn't know if we had made a contribution to the shelter or if we needed to pay on the way out. I raised my eyebrows and shot John a wary look. Riley hid under the worn and hairy sofa we sat on as we recounted his negative behavior: the unprovoked biting, the wild look in his eyes that signaled an attack, his menacing of Cairo and the fact that we never knew what to expect from him.

The behaviorist diagnosed Riley's incidents of aggressive behavior as "evil play attacks." She said that her own cat sat on top of the refrigerator and swatted at her. Was she suggesting that we should tolerate this behavior? She recommended we buy more cat toys and leave them around the house so we could distract Riley when he seemed ready to pounce. We asked if a playmate might be a good solution. She stared at us hard, narrowed her eyes and asked, "Why would you want to get a third cat?"

We left the meeting no better informed than when we arrived. We had no rapport with this woman. "I think she must be better with animals than humans," John said as we stepped into the rainy evening. This was a strong statement coming from a man who rarely said a harsh word about anyone.

"I didn't get anything out of that meeting," I concurred, disappointed that we weren't given a magic pill or even any insight into Riley's perplexing behavior. Were toys really the answer? I pictured our tidy two-story house littered with cat toys. How many playthings would it take to have one within reach whenever Riley threatened? Nevertheless, we dutifully stopped at a pet store on the way home and bought thirty-dollars' worth of cat toys, especially the ones the behaviorist had suggested: Da Bird, a feather toy on a wand to wave in the air to make the bird fly, and Cat Dancer, tiny pieces of cardboard on the end of a wire.

The toys never seemed to be where we needed them when Riley turned ornery, so we resorted to plan B: adopting a third cat. Even before we saw the behaviorist we had been intrigued with the idea of a playmate to dissipate Riley's energy. Cairo had shown no interest in engaging with him so perhaps we could find a better match.

Adding a third cat seemed like an anomaly for our family. John and I had come from families with two children and now we were raising two children. We never considered a third child, but we considered a third cat because of an overriding concern to keep Riley happy. In retrospect, getting a third cat to solve a cat behavior problem seemed like adding a third child to a family to calm a hyperactive child. Grace was an extremely active child and we had never considered having a third child to keep her company.

My cat allergy resurfaced after adopting Cairo. I had relieved my stuffy nose with a steroid nasal spray with one cat in the household, but with two cats the medication did not work as well. A third cat meant we needed to rid our home of as much cat dander as possible. John and I disposed of stuffed furniture, carpets and unnecessary pillows. We encased mattresses and bed pillows in plastic and lined cat beds with towels that we washed weekly. We vacuumed and dusted every Saturday to ensure our home had minimal cat dander.

Not only did we clean the house, but we wiped Riley and Cairo with dander-removing solutions. We were not convinced this was adequate, so we tried to give them showers. We started with docile Cairo. John held her in the shower to wash her. When the shower door opened, Cairo bolted, soaking wet and bedraggled. I waited for her with a towel, but trying to dry a wet, squirming cat is like trying to hold cooked spaghetti. Finally, I blow-dried her fur for a professional finish. John emerged from the shower, covered with scratches.

After that, Cairo ran and hid whenever she heard the shower. Figuring the emotional and physical damage for all parties was not worth the effort, we didn't try to bathe Riley. Instead, we thoroughly cleaned the house every week and deluded ourselves that we were ready to add another cat to our family.

Mismatched

With a plan for channeling Riley's energy, we started to look for a third cat: a one-year-old male that was friendly with both people and other cats. Riley had been a good match for Cairo because they were of opposite genders. For some reason, I forgot this bit of wisdom when I sought a male companion for Riley. Perhaps I was thinking in terms of pairing two boys as playmates. I also thought a younger cat was more likely to be accepted by both Riley and Cairo. Parents of children rarely have the opportunity to predetermine the sex and characteristics of their offspring. You get what you get. Each cat is unique and, like people, some mix with different personalities better than others. We might have had better instincts for choosing a companion for Riley if we had understood him better.

We trooped from shelter to shelter, followed up newspaper ads and scanned Petfinder.com. We drove to nearby towns and ventured into private homes where we waited patiently while enthusiastic foster parents tried to coax feral kittens out of hiding. Very close to Christmas, we met Eastie, who had been found in East Boston. He was a sleek black cat, friendly and alert as he watched us through his cage door. When we took him out of his enclosure, he tried to reach into an adjacent cage to make contact with the cat inside, a gesture I interpreted as being outgoing. He was thin with large round feet and long legs. We thought his big feet were cute, but apparently, as with puppies, they indicated the size he would become.

Eastie had been neutered and cleared for adoption. We took him home that day. We had long discussions about what to name him. We were quite taken with his shiny black coat and played with every word we could conjure that meant "black." We even turned to foreign-language dictionaries. There was Schwarzy (German), Nero (Italian), Negro (Spanish) and Pongo (Maori). And, more typical pet names: Jet, Coal, Onyx, Raven, Inky, Shadow and Sooty. We finally settled on Ebon, short for ebony.

When Ebon arrived, Riley was three years old and starting to settle down; Cairo was eight.

Riley and Cairo enjoyed quiet, predictable lives punctuated by daily walks and the occasional chipmunk conquest. They usually carried their wounded prey into the house where the chipmunks invariably escaped and provided them with much needed entertainment. Riley's periodic attacks were our only concern.

The day we brought Ebon home, we whisked him upstairs and installed him in our guest room for quarantine. In one room, he could adjust to his new surroundings without being overwhelmed by a new house to explore or stressed by two alarmed resident cats. While Ebon occupied the guest room, Riley and Cairo sat in the upstairs hallway, a safe three feet from the guest room door, waiting and listening. They stared at the door with unwavering attention, ears pointed forward. As soon as Ebon caught their scent, he reached his foreleg under the door as far as he could, trying to make contact. They were mesmerized by Ebon's flailing leg, and never made a sound or movement unless to retreat downstairs.

We fed all three cats at the same time on either side of the guest room door to create a positive experience. If a cat associates another cat with something pleasurable, such as food, it is more likely to accept the other feline. The feedings went well and the quarantine period ended, so we took the next step. We separated the cats with a screen barrier so they could see each other without having physical contact. John fashioned a spare aluminum screen door between our family and living rooms.

Ebon sat alone in the living room while the rest of us stayed in the family room; Grace watched television, John and I tapped away on our computers and Riley and Cairo sat several feet away from the door to monitor the newcomer. Ebon looked at us through the screen and cried. He pawed at the door and cried some more. We talked to him, confident that separation was the best thing, but didn't let him into the family room. Suddenly, he leapt through the screen door, bending the frame in the process. John and I were impressed by his strength, but his bravado had the opposite effect on Cairo and Riley. They shrank to the sides of the room, clearly horrified.

We hustled Ebon back upstairs to avoid any conflicts. The following evening, we trashed the bent screen and dusted off the four-foot-square cage that had been sitting in our basement. We installed Ebon in the cage and rolled it into the family room so he could join the rest of us. After an hour of watching him pace and listening to him howl, we declared him acclimated and gave him his freedom.

Ebon's drive to interact and play was unrelenting. The cage that had jailed him was now a mountain to explore. The same energy that sent him through the screen door had him repeatedly running over to Cairo, ready to pounce, not once or twice, but ten times in a row. Although Riley loved to play, he also refused to engage with Ebon. In our multistory house, Ebon liked to race down the steps, make a one hundred eighty-degree turn into the living room, sprint through the family room and hurtle through the cat door. For the return trip he blasted through the cat flap again to race to his starting position at the top of the stairs. Cairo and Riley stood in stunned wonder. Ebon was like a locomotive barreling through our home and their lives.

As energetic as Ebon was, we suspected that he had been low on the pecking order as a kitten. He always hung back at dinnertime, as if he had learned to wait until the others were finished. John fed the cats in the order we had acquired them, saying their names as he put their food down. Ebon was fed last, although he always finished first. As Cairo and Riley nibbled their food, he patiently sat behind them until they finished and walked away. Then he sauntered over and inhaled what they had left in the bottom of their bowls. Riley and Cairo preferred grazing throughout the day, but with Ebon around that was not an option. Ebon ate any food we offered him, including mushrooms and kale chips.

Ebon's willingness to eat anything might have gotten him into trouble before he entered the shelter. He drank huge amounts of water and peed quantities to match while isolated in our guest room. Our vet, Dr. Peterson, drew blood and concluded that he had kidney damage. She speculated that he had scavenged something poisonous as a hungry stray.

Dr. Peterson had been a source of comfort when we were struggling with the illness and death of our first cat, Steve. In that same time period, she had owned a terminally ill dog, so we were in similar emotional circumstances. Ebon's kidney problem was discovered soon after we brought him home, so she recommended that we return him to the shelter. Our eyes widened.

"You may have to inject liquid under his skin every day, and I just don't want to see you go through this so soon after your experience with Steve," she said. We appreciated her sensitivity, but in the few weeks Ebon had been in our home, we found his personality so engaging that we totally rejected the idea of returning him. We liked his playfulness. His favorite toy was a mouse that dangled from a stick. He was confident and friendly; he wanted to connect with us. He had energy and pluck. True to his spunky nature, Ebon rebounded and his blood work was normal within a month.

After Ebon burst on to the scene, Riley retreated to his basket and hibernated for the winter. Cairo dealt with the intruder as best she could by hissing and seeking refuge under chairs and low tables. Ebon tried to engage her by jumping on her back or throwing his front leg over her shoulders, all requests that she refused with a hiss. He relentlessly chased her. We were powerless to stop him. "It's good exercise for Cairo," John rationalized.

Six months after Ebon's arrival, Riley began a campaign to take back his territory. He had been the dominant cat before Ebon arrived. Cairo was so timid she never offered Riley any competition. Riley chased Ebon around the house to reestablish his dominance, but, by this time, Ebon had filled out and matured into a muscular sixteen-pound cat, outweighing Riley by five pounds.

Ebon seemed surprised and bewildered by Riley's aggression. Ebon had a happy-go-lucky demeanor and an innocence that were charming. He was also a little clumsy, which garnered our sympathy. When he jumped onto a counter, sometimes his hind legs lagged behind and he stumbled to right himself. His awkwardness reminded me of Baby Huey, a character from 1950s comic books: a gigantic, naïve duckling that other ducklings excluded from their play.

Cairo and Riley ignored Ebon, making it very clear they did not like him. They never played with him and met his advances with swatting or hissing. Riley regularly stalked Ebon and cornered him. Ebon eventually submitted to Riley's dominance. Many times, we heard Riley's wavering cry of sovereignty from another room. Each time we rushed to see what was going on, we found Ebon lying on his back, cowering, his head hunkered down as Riley stood glaring at him, ears flat against his head.

Our cats had established their pecking order: Riley was dominant, Ebon was next and then Cairo, who didn't want anything to do with either of them. Although second in command, Ebon's natural confidence and pluck kept him looking for someone or something to dominate. Most of the time it was Cairo, but my full-sized stuffed Labrador retriever became another of his victims. The first time Ebon saw the dog, he stopped, sized it up, then lunged and bit it on the neck. It fell over. He had conquered.

Animosity between the two male cats developed into territorial battles. I found sticky yellow liquid on windows, windowsills, under beds and on a jewelry box atop my bureau. I believed this was Riley's urine because I remembered finding dried liquid spots under Henry's bed soon after Riley had been quarantined in his room. And one cat had clawed the bed sheet into shreds, as way of marking with the pads of his feet.

Ebon tried to carve out territory in the kitchen by spraying the toaster, microwave, electrical outlets and kitchen walls with urine. We found puddles of urine on the kitchen counter and on the dining room and basement floors.

Eventually the entire house was a war zone as both parties marked as much territory as they could: drapes, radiator covers, doll display cases, lampshades, photo albums, the clothes dryer, power saws, stained glass windows, the grandfather clock, a toilet, tote bags, a waste basket, the laundry sink, a room humidifier and—my favorite—a small chest of plastic drawers filled with screws.

We were at our wits' ends. Each day that I found more evidence of urine marking, my heart sank. I cleaned and scrubbed, but some things had to be thrown out. "I'm throwing out this humidifier," I told John. Ever frugal, he objected, insisting it could be cleaned.

"There are too many small parts. It will always smell. It could be a health issue. I'm getting rid of it," I said.

The toaster was discarded, too. John went through his drawers of screws and pulled out the rusty ones, rinsed out the drawers and replaced them after everything dried. I pulled sticky books off shelves, wiped, dried and returned them to their places after cleaning the shelf. We didn't want to live like this. We needed to find a solution to our cats' behavior.

◆ ◆ ◆

When our children were growing up I often felt like I was raising children at opposite ends of the personality spectrum. Henry was an introvert who spent a lot of time in his room on the computer while Grace was out of the house at soccer practice or with friends. As different as they were, they led their separate lives without much conflict. Now we were parenting two cats with very different personalities that were creating havoc.

A Behaviorist with Credentials: BVMS, DACVA, DACVB

We sought professional help again to solve our cat problem. This time we chose a nationally known animal behaviorist. I had read one of Dr. Baylor's books on dog behavior and watched him in a PBS television special. Our cat sitter warned us that he had a reputation for using drugs to change pet behavior, but I wanted to hear him out. The price tag was high, but the care seemed thorough. For a set fee we would have an initial consultation and six months of follow-up email care. Before the consultation, Dr. Baylor required us to take Riley, the presumed problem pet, to our local vet to make sure there were no underlying medical issues. We filled out nine-page questionnaires on all three cats before bringing them to the clinic so the vet could observe them.

I drove more than an hour to the clinic in western Massachusetts. John worked nearby, so he met me there on the day of our appointment. I had to get three cats in their carriers and into the car by myself. It was challenging. My tried and true method of crating a cat was to create a comfy towel bed in the carrier, lace it with catnip and place a trail of cat treats on the floor leading into the carrier. Always tempted by food, Ebon walked into his carrier. I zipped it closed. Riley was curious but needed a push. Cairo stuck out all four legs, clinging to the sides of her carrier, making it nearly impossible to stuff her in. However, I triumphed and confined her like the others.

I wanted to make sure the cats were happy for the long trip, so I poked more cat treats and toys through the carriers' wire mesh doors. I put the crates containing Riley and Ebon on the floor in the back of my car for security and stability, then leveled off the front seat for Cairo's carrier and belted her in. Because of the added time it took to corral Cairo, we started late. As I drove, I talked to the cats, "Here we go, guys. Are you comfortable? I'm going around a curve here. OK, we'll be on the highway soon. Why are you crying, Cairo? It's OK." The more I talked, the more they cried. Part way through the trip, one of the cats started to make coughing sounds. It happened intermittently, but eventually stopped. "Everything must be OK, right?" I said to myself. I ignored the little voice in my head that suggested otherwise.

At the clinic complex, I pulled into parking lot after parking lot trying to find the specific clinic. When I finally found the correct one, I pulled Ebon's crate from the car only to discover he had vomited multiple times. I climbed into the backseat of my compact station wagon and took him out of the carrier to remove the towel soaked with vomit. There was also vomit matted in his fur. When I checked on Riley, I saw that he had also been carsick and, like Ebon, had vomit in his coat. I put both cats back into their carriers, got out of the car and threw the dirty towels and toys into the closest trashcan.

I spoke reassuringly to the cats, but I could have used some reassurance myself at this point. I grabbed the two cat carriers and rushed into the clinic, looking frantically for John. He was usually early to every appointment, but that day he was nowhere to be found. I ran to the receptionist and said, "My name is Linda Patterson and we have an appointment with Dr. Baylor at three, but my cats got sick in the car and I have to clean them up. I have to leave these two cats here while I go get the third one from the car so if my husband comes, will you let him know?" The receptionist seemed nonplussed so I carried Riley and Ebon back to the waiting room and stacked their carriers against the wall. I hurried back to the car to get Cairo.

I was panting when I returned to the waiting room with her and spotted John. In a huff, I set Cairo's carrier down beside him and said, "Guard Cairo and check in with the receptionist while I clean up Riley and Ebon."

I picked up the other two carriers and bumped my way into the restroom. The cats stepped warily from their carriers and I snapped on their leashes. It was a relatively small room with only two stalls, so I didn't have to cover much ground to catch them if they bolted. Dazed from carsickness, they cooperated as I washed them off with paper towels. I wiped out their carriers, lured them back in and emerged from the ladies' room flushed and exasperated.

Dr. Baylor was late, which gave me a chance to decompress. When it was our turn, a vet tech ushered us into a sizable room with a desk at one end. Dr. Baylor sat on the corner of the desk, four young veterinary students in white coats sitting in a line to his right. A veterinary resident from Japan sat closest to him. We were offered two seats in the middle of the room facing the vet. It felt like we were being interrogated. We opened the carriers and the cats emerged. Riley sought the highest location in the room, on a file cabinet, but Ebon was so sick he reentered his carrier and stayed there for the duration of the visit. Cairo found middle ground, close to her carrier.

Dr. Baylor impressed us. He maintained constant eye contact as we recounted our story and he answered each of our questions. Ms. Okabe, the Japanese resident, took notes. She was our contact for further consultation.

The vet thought Riley was high-strung and had status issues. When Ebon joined the family, Riley felt compelled to mark his territory, which was essentially our entire house. Neighborhood cats that visited our yard may have contributed to Riley's anxiety. When he saw them through the window he urine-marked the glass panes.

Dr. Baylor speculated that the puddles in the basement were also from Riley because he did not like our cat litter and found other places to toilet. It was important for him, as the dominant cat, to pee in obvious places such as countertops, the dining room floor, etc., so that everyone would know where he had peed. He had never covered up his feces so this sounded like consistent behavior. He had even defecated in our laundry tub in the basement.

Dr. Baylor instructed us to buy four new cat boxes and to fill three of them with different levels of a sandy litter. The fourth contained the old litter as a control. As directed, we varied the depth of the sandy litter and isolated Riley to see which box he preferred. The test did not reveal any strong preference, so we reasoned that Riley's insecurity and desire to dominate his territory motivated his peeing in inappropriate places.

Dr. Baylor put Riley on Prozac. As the dosage slowly increased, we sensed a difference in our cat. He seemed unstable, disheveled, stressed, confused and delicate. His temper was shorter. When awake he continued to perch on the highest spot in a room, but he started sleeping under a small, low table, a protected place. His behavior was unpredictable. Once, when he passed Ebon in the hall, Ebon playfully pounced on him. Riley's reaction was extreme. He chased Ebon upstairs and cornered him. A vicious fight ensued and they littered our upstairs hall with tufts of fur.

Dr. Baylor suggested we buy a black light to reveal cat urine since it is invisible in daylight. As we crept through the dark following the purplish light, we were appalled to find many more items than expected marked with urine. We found long streaks of urine on a couch, sections of radiators that glowed and many more walls than anticipated with long, liquid drips.

After identifying all signs of cat urine, we followed the vet's instructions and scrubbed each stain with Pine-Sol three times, then sprayed it with Zero Odor to erase the scent. John and I worked well as a team, checking in with each other as we crawled around the house. "Did you get everything in the living room? What about the other couch?" John asked.

"My knees are killing me," I whined. "I can't believe we didn't know all this was here. This is disgusting. How did we not smell this?" We were oblivious to the smell after living for so long in a house saturated with cat urine. We needed to remove all traces of the odor because cats are sensitive to their own scent and will respray the same place as soon as it fades.

After a few months the urine marking eased, but Riley was still on edge. He constantly stared aggressively at Ebon, however he was less aggressive with us. The tension was palpable. Things were better, but we were still not comfortable. Nine months after meeting this behaviorist, despite his credentials, we tried another.

Round Three

Our cat sitter worked in an animal shelter and recommended our third behaviorist. This one, she assured us, was particularly good with cats. Again, we filled out forms, loaded the three cats into the car and drove into Boston. As with earlier car trips, we had to clean up Riley and Ebon after bouts of carsickness before presenting them to the new doctor.

Dr. D'Angelo, a friendly, middle-aged woman, was easy to talk to and we immediately had good rapport with her. When we sent her a picture of the cats eating together she replied, "Thanks for the picture! You guys are awesome. I can already tell I am going to love working with you." We were off on the right foot.

She suggested we start Riley on a drug called Buspirone, which had been reported to make some animals friendlier. This sounded good. It would be wonderful to have cats that cuddled with each other and enjoyed playing together. Dr. D'Angelo slowly tapered Riley's Prozac and started him on Buspirone. He took it for six months before we concluded that it had no effect on his behavior. We weaned him off the drug and resumed giving him Prozac.

Initially, Dr. D'Angelo suggested we separate the male cats for two weeks. We put Ebon in the basement and left Riley and Cairo upstairs. Ebon clawed at the basement door and cried piteously until we realized he suffered from the isolation. We switched Riley and Cairo to the basement. Riley was accustomed to eating in the basement because we had fed him there for a while to prevent Ebon from eating his Prozac-laced food. Cairo wasn't content to stay in the basement and frequently took her chances upstairs where Ebon might jump on her. When he bothered her too much, she retreated back to the basement. We realized this situation would not work in the long run: The cats either suffered from being away from us or being close to each other.

Dr. D'Angelo offered email consultation and phone call-in time each week. After months of back and forth, she summed up our situation by saying, "Riley and Ebon do not like each other and never will. The best-case scenario is to re-home Riley, but I know that is out of the question for you. You need to split your house into two territories to keep the cats apart." Riley was presumed to be the problem pet, but he was part of our family. Dr. D'Angelo was correct: We would not find another home for Riley or send him to a farm. We would find another solution.

Splitting our house into two territories was a surprising but intriguing prescription. Dr. D'Angelo asked us to send her a sketch of our home's floor plan, so John mailed her the architect's drawings and his own sketch. We were skeptical that we could split our house comfortably or that this solution would solve our cat problem. But we were creative people and loved solving problems. Not every house can be split into two distinct spaces, but we were willing to try.

After conferring with the vet, we came to the same conclusion: We could install a door between our family room and kitchen. Unfortunately, this was the busiest thoroughfare in our home. As a trial, we blocked the doorway for a month with a piece of plywood. Eventually, we hung a permanent glass door. This new solution provided one male cat the run of the upstairs, living room and family room and the other male cat the run of the kitchen, dining room and basement. To ward off boredom, every other day we switched them to the other space. In retrospect it seems illogical. Cats want their own territory and spray to mark it, but forcing one cat to stay in the basement all the time was not fair. We found the key to minimizing the spraying and fighting was to keep Riley and Ebon apart. They still had some contact when they ate together in the kitchen, but that didn't seem to be a problem. Cairo protected herself from Ebon by slipping between territories whenever the door opened. This new arrangement kept the peace, despite being highly inconvenient.

SLOWING DOWN
IN NORTH CAROLINA

Shifting Landscape

A few months after we started working with Dr. D'Angelo, John learned that his company was transferring him to North Carolina. Since he was close to retirement age, we decided he should keep the job and make the move. We made a wish list for a house—two-car garage, double sinks in the bathroom, screened porch—and, most importantly, a house that could be split into two cat territories.

We sat in an Italian restaurant after a long day of house-hunting in North Carolina and reviewed our list of possibilities. "You know, John, we can't buy that house you and the real estate agent like. It has casement windows. You can't put cat doors in casement windows. We need a house with double-hung windows so you can install cat doors like you did at home."

John leaned back and exploded, "I'm not buying a house based on cats!" My eyes widened. It was difficult to believe this was the same man who was so devoted to our cats. He took them for walks on leashes, installed cat doors and outdoor cages and rushed to their aid whenever he heard feline discord.

After a night's rest, reason prevailed and we continued our search, eventually finding the perfect house to divide into two sections. We bought a French door, John installed it and the house was ready for our cats.

I stayed in Massachusetts to sell our home, but our daughter Grace and I helped John move the cats and all their paraphernalia—litter boxes, scratching posts, sleep baskets, food dishes and toys—to Raleigh. A two-day road trip with carsick cats was out of the question, so we booked plane tickets. Each cat needed to be accompanied by an adult on the plane. Grace was living on her own at this point, and wanted to see our new house. The trip echoed our new normal for travel: Riley and Ebon threw up on the way to the airport, I switched out the towels lining their carriers before boarding the plane and Cairo cried the entire time. Fortunately, the plane was not full and our animal-loving flight attendant encouraged us to make the cats comfortable in their carriers on the extra seats.

When we arrived at the new house, we put down the carriers in the silent, empty country kitchen and opened the wire carrier doors. Ebon stepped out first. He looked around and plunked down in the middle of the floor. Much later, Riley and Cairo emerged. The house held new scents, especially because we had installed new parquet flooring. After some preliminary sniffing, Riley and Cairo retreated to top shelves in the pantry where they stayed for hours. Only food brought them down at the end of the day.

This house was neutral territory because the cats arrived at the same time. None had precedence because he or she had lived there longer. John installed one cat door in a window that led to a screened porch and the other in a window that led to a deck where he set up a wire cage. This allowed the cats to survey the woods behind our house and occasionally spot a deer or chipmunk. They could catch the earthy smells on a breeze and listen to songbirds and the cries of hawks. I attached a birdfeeder to a window so they could watch the birds (and squirrels) eating. From the screened porch, they could enjoy the smell of a rainstorm and stay dry. They had options and entertainment.

We lived in this home for more than two years before we realized that spraying, albeit discreet, had resumed. As I walked by the dining room one day I smelled a familiar and undeniable odor. Upon inspection I found a puddle in the corner, discoloring the parquet flooring beneath it. We scrubbed the area repeatedly and sprayed with a chemical John had ordered on the Internet. A few days later, someone refreshed the urine. There was no way of getting the smell out. The urine had seeped into the cracks between the one-inch pieces of wood making up the parquet. After we had the offending blocks of wood replaced, I used a small stool as a barricade, wedged into place by an iron floor lamp. I was determined to protect this corner from further cat spraying.

Once again, we crept around our house in the dark with a black light. This survey revealed some splashes in other parts of the house, particularly the bedspreads in the guest room. Riley often slept in this room and probably considered it his turf. Although the linens had been laundered and there was no odor, I warned our son, Henry, to keep the door closed when he visited. He was confident there would be no problem, but I caught the waft of a distinct feline odor while standing in the guest room doorway one day. I asked my son if the smell bothered him, but he noticed nothing. I didn't say anything more, but I am sure Riley left his mark because the odor disappeared when my son's luggage was gone.

Regulating Riley

We had come a long way since Riley was first prescribed liquid Prozac. John used to wrestle this squirmy cat into a stronghold each morning to squirt tuna-flavored Prozac down his throat. Riley put up such a fight that we moved his dosing time to dinner so John and I could work as a team. One of us held him while the other wedged the eyedropper between Riley's teeth. With his mouth clamped shut, Riley swung his head from side to side. Mixing the liquid Prozac into his food didn't work for very long either. Prozac has a strong smell, and apparently a ghastly taste.

Dr. Peterson, in Boston, suggested Pill Pockets: doughy cat treats with a hollow for hiding pills. We pushed the bottle of pricey Prozac to the back of the refrigerator, filled a prescription for Prozac tablets and bought a bag of Pill Pockets.

At dinner the next night, John tucked Riley's Prozac pill into the chewy cat treat. "You're going to love this, Riley," he said. And Riley gobbled it down.

When we moved to North Carolina, we brought the Pill Pockets with us. Riley seemed to look forward to them. We learned to make a big show of preparing the Pill Pocket by shaking the bag, putting the tiny white pill inside the treat and rolling it into a ball between our palms. We needed to do this before dishing out wet cat food for all three cats. Once Riley smelled the fishy odor of his favorite cat food— and he would only eat one kind, Friskies Classic Seafood Entrée—he was not interested in the Pill Pocket. As soon as he ate his medicine, we put down the cats' food bowls.

I once made the mistake of preparing the Pill Pocket out of Riley's sight. When I dropped it in front of him he looked at it, then up at me as if to say, "What's this?" I had to take it back, shake the bag and make big hand motions, as if I were rolling the treat into a ball, before he would eat it.

Pill Pockets are a wonderful product, but at some point our bags contained dry and crumbly pockets instead of the usual soft and chewy ones we were used to. We had stockpiled six bags of the new ones before we realized this. At this point, Riley refused to eat his predinner treats.

Riley's refusal to eat his pill fueled our creativity.

"Success!" John crowed one day. "I got Riley to take his pill by smearing the Pill Pocket with margarine." This worked a few times, but then Riley balked again.

I started experimenting. "I rolled the Pill Pocket in margarine *and* catnip, and he ate it!" I said. It was like a congenial ping-pong match.

Riley ate these embellished treats for a while, but then abruptly stopped. When we dropped the embellished pill in front of him, he just looked at us. The other cats sat and watched this routine every night, knowing they would not eat until Riley downed his treat. While their dinner was delayed, we had to be vigilant that one of the other cats didn't gobble down the tidbit with the Prozac pill.

In a desperate experiment we used a spring-loaded pill shooter to pop the pill down Riley's throat. John gripped Riley while I tried to pry open his mouth, insert the pill shooter and push the plunger. Riley was so wriggly I could never get the six-inch-long instrument positioned correctly or, if I managed to push the plunger, the pill fell out of his mouth.

Then, we tried hiding the pill in his cat food. This worked for a couple of days.

"I think he smells it," John said.

I cut the tiny white pill into smaller pieces and hid them in the food, thinking the smell of smaller pieces would be easier to disguise. That worked for a couple of nights. I doubled my efforts. I took a little cat food, rolled it into a ball like a meatball and tucked the pill inside. Then I crushed a cat treat and rolled the cat food ball in the treat. He ate it.

My next variation consisted of crushing two cat treats and adding catnip. Another night I crushed the Prozac and dissolved it in the liquid from a can of tuna. Riley ate that. The next night when I mixed his pill with a dab of tuna, he refused it. After that, John tried cutting the pill into small pieces and feeding Riley one small piece at breakfast, another at dinner and another at snack time. We were writing notes that said, "Riley ate a piece of pill at breakfast, but not dinner and snack, so I think he got a third of his dose." A few days of that and we realized that the arithmetic was too difficult to track.

We took an analytical approach. "What seemed to work best?" we asked ourselves.

Riley loved cheese, so one weekend we decided to buy Velveeta cheese, a soft food we could hide the pill in. On Monday, John was electric with his news. "So, I cut the pill into quarters and then I made a bunch of little balls of Velveeta. I gave Ebon and Cairo each a ball of cheese and when Riley saw them eating the cheese, I gave him the cheese with the pills. He ate them!"

Three days later, Riley realized that the cheese contained his pills. We tried to win back his trust by feeding him cheese without pills, but he would have none of it. In fact, he refused any wet food that we offered, including his favorite Classic Seafood Entrée. He wanted dry food. So, we gave him kibble. And, we gave up trying to feed him Prozac.

Perplexed

I sat on a stool at my kitchen counter one Sunday morning sipping coffee. The sun streamed through the windows creating light designs across the wood floor and cabinetry. It was my favorite time of day in this room. I felt contemplative. My gaze shifted from the light play to my beautiful gray Riley who sat quietly on the floor.

I felt worn down by Riley's repeated refusal to take his Prozac. He had taken it for three years and was on it for two reasons: He sprayed our home after we adopted Ebon and he attacked us and the other cats. Now that we had moved to a new house in North Carolina, the spraying was minimal. I theorized that the new house represented neutral ground, so he didn't need to mark his territory as much as he had in Boston. The aggression, still a problem at times, seemed worse when Riley was hungry. Could we control it with constant feeding? I decided to trust Riley's instinct to leave Prozac behind.

I knew that Prozac needed to be tapered when terminating use. Since Riley had been getting a partial dose for a week or so despite our best efforts, we rationalized that this was adequate for ramping down his dosage. Weeks after he stopped taking Prozac, his personality seemed to change. He became affectionate and wanted to be with us all the time. He gazed lovingly at John and competed with Cairo for the spot on his lap. Cairo had always perched precariously on John's thin, muscular thighs as he watched TV. She looked uncomfortable, but she was determined to be with him. Although now affectionate, Riley's dominance continued. All he needed to do was approach and stare at Cairo and she would slink off to sleep in a basket. Riley sat on John's chest and frantically kneaded the base of his neck with his claws retracted. After kneading, he sat next to John, purring as he draped his forelegs over John's thighs.

Riley cried piteously at our bedroom door at night because he wanted to stay with us at bedtime. We allowed this one time. He had a shorter sleep cycle than we did, and entertained himself by leaping onto bureaus and knocking objects to the floor. We soon banished him to the kitchen where we couldn't hear his cries.

When Riley wanted to be fed during the day, he stared at me. He sat next to my desk and kept a steady gaze on me, following my movements. I usually fed him immediately, even if it was inconvenient. He never gained weight so there didn't seem to be a problem with managing his behavior this way. We kept a bowl of dry food in the cupboard ready to serve. As soon as Riley ate his fill, we picked it up so the other cats didn't overfeed. They *would* gain weight.

We learned not to overstimulate Riley by petting him too long as one way to control his aggression. As soon as we saw Riley staring, pawing, attacking or growling at the other cats, we put him in time-out in a small bathroom. John was convinced he had a mental issue and frequently said, "Riley is having trouble with his demons today."

One evening, as I said goodnight to Riley, he ran through the kitchen doorway and down the hall. I caught up with him and slid my hands under his belly, noting with satisfaction that he had gained a little weight. Back in the kitchen area he jumped on the brown leather couch and started to knead a rust-colored velour pillow. I took this away and patted the towel at the end of the couch where he usually slept next to the arm. He didn't budge.

There was something about his demeanor that warned me to be careful. I walked behind the couch to put something between us and proceeded to the door. I felt the claws and teeth on the back of my upper thigh and knew immediately he had bitten a hole in my new pants. He glowered at me from the floor, ready to spring again. I pointed my right forefinger at him and said in a stern voice, "No!" As he quickened, ready to spring again, I shouted, "No!" again. I started to turn the light out and walk the five steps to the door, but rethought my strategy. I left the light on, watching him the entire time, hurried to the door and slipped into the living room, pulling the glass door closed.

Back in my bedroom, I pulled off my black knit pants and saw a small hole of light where fabric should have been. John confirmed that I was bleeding from long scratches on the back of my leg. I washed my wound, my husband applied antiseptic ointment and we discussed what to do. A new vet had written Riley a prescription for Xanax, an antianxiety medicine, in case we needed it. He said it would take the edge off. The next morning, I walked straight into my home office, found the prescription and made it number one on my to-do list. Grimly I thought, "Here we go again."

Xanax lasted one night. After twelve hours on the drug, Riley was uncontrollable. He raced back and forth on the kitchen counter at dinnertime. I used to be so proud of his self-control when I prepared his dinner. He knew exactly where he was allowed to sit on the desk at the end of the counter. Sometimes he would push the limit by putting his front paws on the edge of the counter as if to get a better view of food preparation, but he always showed restraint even as I poured the dry food in the bowl or scooped wet food from a can. Tonight, he was a different cat. We felt sad for him because clearly he was not in control of himself. We vowed never to give him Xanax again. In fact, we never used that vet again.

Months passed and one morning after watching Riley run from the bathroom to the closet to the bedroom and down the hall and back a couple of times, I thought, "It's like having a toddler with ADHD." This small soul needed help.

Our new vet, Dr. Sametz, mentioned a Prozac cream that we could rub on the inside of Riley's ear. John was ambivalent about starting Riley on Prozac again despite the challenges of living with him. Riley had grown so attached to

John that when John put on his hat and coat to go outside, Riley lashed out at him and ran away. John liked the new, devoted Riley so much that he was incredibly tolerant of his attacks.

I won out and we ordered the Prozac ointment. Not only did it work but we got the best of both Rileys, the one on Prozac and the one not on Prozac. He continued to be affectionate, and his playful self reemerged as he tossed a catnip mouse around. He still remained on high alert watching Ebon, but cat arguments were less frequent and rarely evolved into fur-flying wrestling matches. Riley no longer needed to eat hourly, but we continued to feed him on demand to be safe. He rarely ate during the day so at bedtime we closed him in one part of the house away from the other cats and gave him a large bowl of dry cat food to nibble during the night. The new formulation of Prozac stabilized him and we all settled into a more satisfying routine.

◆ ◆ ◆

Our entire family reaped the benefits of working with behavior professionals. In addition to cat behaviorists, we had worked with a family psychologist after Grace arrived. Once she emerged from toddlerhood, life calmed down, but her teenage years were trying. Like Riley, she was helped by medication. By the time she graduated from high school, medication allowed her to be on the honor roll and win numerous awards for her athletic and leadership abilities.

Like Riley, Henry hated taking pills. Unfortunately I was never as sympathetic with him as I was with Riley. I remember making six-year-old Henry sit in the middle of the hall floor for more than an hour insisting he swallow a pill. He was easier to reason with than a cat. I don't remember who won out, but he survived his illness. To this day, he struggles to down pills.

A Complicated Cat

Before Riley was on Prozac, we had always thought of him as the villain in our household of cats. Ebon was easygoing and friendly, and Cairo was a complete innocent who tried to stay out of everyone's way. Our assumption was tested when we moved from Boston to North Carolina. While packing, we discovered an old video clip shot soon after Ebon came to live with us. In the video, he stands on his hind legs to reach the top of the table where Riley is sleeping in a basket. He bats at Riley, who wakes with a confused look before tucking his head back under his paw. When Ebon attacks again, Riley is on alert and bats back with spits and growls. Ebon then jumps up on the table to make a full-frontal attack. Fascinated, we caught this on videotape like amateur journalists, being careful not to interfere with the action. Over the years we had forgotten this event. Despite this, we had never thought of Ebon as a bully.

Ebon was full of contradictions. He had grown into a tall, stately cat exuding confidence, but he could be easily cowed. If the doorbell rang, he ran to the door to meet the stranger, but if he heard a loud noise in the house, he hid. Outdoors on his leash, he fearlessly tromped through deep leaves looking for prey and marking his territory. When the leash stretched taut, he came back to rub my legs, as if to reconnect. He chased Riley under tables and chairs when out of sorts, but, more often, he lay on his back, feet in the air, as he submitted to Riley's dominating stares and warning cries.

The first time our Boston vet met Ebon she exclaimed, "What a confident cat!" He was out of his carrier, all sixteen pounds of him sprawled in the middle of the exam room floor, looking completely relaxed. His demeanor quickly changed as she prodded and poked during the exam. Although easygoing at home, he was not shy about using his teeth to communicate and had never learned to retract his claws when pawing for attention. The vet tech took him into the back room to draw blood and urine as John and I settled into the waiting room. When the tech returned thirty minutes later, she said they were not able to get a urine sample and described Ebon as "vicious."

"Not our Ebon!" we exclaimed in disbelief. After that first visit, the staff was wary of him.

Soon after we moved to the house in North Carolina, he pushed through the screening on the porch, jumped more than ten feet to the ground, and explored the woods for a few hours. He rarely vocalized at that age, but when I discovered he had escaped and frantically called him, he cried back, echoing my calls. He followed my voice back to our house and flopped down on the porch's brick floor, his belly heaving for fifteen minutes. He was extremely anxious about something; perhaps he had discovered an unfamiliar animal in the woods. Maybe he was unnerved by being lost in a new environment.

As he became used to our North Carolina home, Ebon grew more confident outdoors and developed a territorial attitude. One afternoon as John walked him up our driveway on a leash, a buck watched and paralleled them from the neighbor's yard. When the deer crossed to our yard and approached, Ebon lunged. The buck screamed and ran away. Ebon tried to chase him, but John held him back.

Another day when John and I took Ebon and Riley out on leashes, we met a neighbor walking his dog. Riley walked up and sniffed the dog's nose. After a pause, Riley arched his back, fluffed his tail and backed away. Ebon, always uncomfortable around dogs, was spooked and started a high-pitched yowl. John quickly picked him up and started down the driveway toward our house. Riley reacted to the alarm in Ebon's voice and rushed after them as Ebon screeched from John's shoulder. I had Riley on the leash and walked as fast as I could to keep up. The faster John walked, the faster Riley trotted close behind and the louder Ebon screamed. As soon as we reached the house we put the cats in separate rooms. It took Ebon hours to calm down. Cat behavior can be baffling, but we surmised that Ebon had transferred his fear of the dog onto Riley: The closer Riley followed John and Ebon, the more Ebon panicked.

Although the new house started as neutral territory, Riley eventually claimed our bedroom, the guest room, the living room and the dining room. He allowed Ebon to use the cat box in the bathroom, sleep in our home office, venture down the hall and hang out in the kitchen. Cairo was welcome anywhere as long as she didn't offend. Ebon started to beg to go into the attached garage more and more. We guessed that Riley's quiet tyranny forced Ebon to claim the garage as his only territory. When Riley tried to take this, too, by spraying my car, I was angry and banned him from Ebon's hideout. Ebon spent hours in the dark space where he often perched on the warm hood of my car or the minivan's roof to look out the garage window. The house may have been Riley's kingdom, but Ebon had a fiefdom where he held his own as a dignified second fiddle.

Cat Infoodtainment

As the cats grew older, their lives became placid. Life was more predictable now that Riley was on Prozac again and Ebon had his own territory. Every morning I sat on a stool at the kitchen island reading the newspaper and drinking coffee as Ebon sat on a stool facing me. Riley perched on the kitchen counter and stared at both of us. Ebon always reached over and tapped my arm with his paw. I rubbed his head. Each time my attention veered back to the paper, he tapped. I rubbed between his shoulders and stroked his head over and over. Even though he clearly craved this attention, he nipped at my fingers as I caressed his face. I stopped petting him, assuming he was overstimulated or I had touched a spot he didn't like. He continued tapping. After many rounds of tapping, petting, tapping, petting, nipping, he jumped down and wandered off.

John fed the cats at five o'clock each morning when he was working. If he slept in, Ebon clawed the bottom of our bedroom door, waiting for John to dress and make his way to the kitchen. I got up around eight o'clock, three hours after the cats had eaten. I danced around to avoid Ebon as he wove in and out of my ankles while I fixed my breakfast. Each morning, I put the yolk from my hard-cooked egg into Ebon's dish because I avoided fat and cholesterol. I stopped doing this when I noticed his sides bulging. Months after I no longer shared the yolk with him, he ran to my side if he heard me crack an egg on the edge of the sink.

By lunchtime, Ebon was always looking for food again. When our children were small, we sent them to daycare while John and I worked. Entertaining small children was not my forte, but here I was with a cat that required stimulation. He would get a walk outside at the end of the day, but he needed indoor opportunities like playing with a laser pointer, fishing out treats from the holes in a wooden box or going on a scavenger hunt.

From time to time, I grabbed a bag of cat snacks and strode to the dining room, shutting the French doors behind me. Ebon and Riley stood on the other side of the glass doors, watching my every move. Cairo slept a lot these days and napped in the living room on her favorite chair.

I balanced the tiny snacks between the vertical spindles on the chair seats in the dining room or next to the chair legs on the floor: ten hiding spots in all. Then I opened the door and Ebon and Riley rushed in, ready to go to work. Ebon headed for the chairs but didn't home in on the treats right away. Typically, he sniffed the length of the spindles but did not find any tidbits. He smelled the center of a chair leg, lifted his nose to the seat, and looked around. Then, he sniffed down the leg, missing the spot where a treat rested. Riley stood and watched. Taking a whiff of air, he rarely located the food either. Ebon usually found the treat, knocked it to the floor with his paw and ate it. Riley always appeared bemused and walked over to me as if he knew I was the true source of cat treats.

Ebon always continued to work the room but not in any logical pattern that I could detect. It reminded me of watching the activity around an ant pile. The ants operated by some plan, yet I couldn't figure it out. Riley and Ebon zeroed in on the runners of a child's oak rocking chair made by my grandfather. Riley caught the scent and nosed a treat on to the floor, his only haul of the day. Ebon slowly checked the chairs in random order, following the updrafts of fish and meat odors, and in the end scarfed most of the snacks.

Watching the cats was a Zen experience, like taking them for walks. Their progress was painstakingly slow. I usually left them on their own for a while and checked back later. I was always amazed to see they had found all the treats. By now it was time for another nap and they wandered off to find a spot in the cat tree or on the floor to soak up sunshine. As usual, Cairo did not stir. I shuffled off to my office or another part of the house where I hoped to have a few hours to myself before Ebon started his dinner campaign.

Losing Cairo

John was careful not to show preference so he always said, "Cairo, you are my favorite female cat." He was protective and made allowances for her. His desk chair was covered with her fur because she liked sleeping there, whether or not he sat with her. When they were both in the chair, John sat on the front edge to avoid disturbing her. As she aged into her teens and became confused, John woke her each night to eat dinner by bringing a food dish to her nose so she could smell it. Only then did she rouse herself and follow him back to the kitchen. She had always slept a lot, but now she slept more and more and ate less and less.

She and John enjoyed sitting on the couch together while John watched the evening news. One night he noticed she was breathing rapidly. He counted her respiration rate at thirty-five to forty breaths per minute. He looked up normal cat respiration rate on the Internet and found that it is twenty to thirty breaths per minute.

The next day, we took Cairo to the vet. Dr. Sametz said, "Cairo's heart is not beating, it's fluttering. She has fluid in her lungs and congestive heart failure." With a long needle she tried to draw off the fluid, but Cairo squirmed and fought the procedure. "Cairo might not live long and I am going to prescribe a blood thinner to minimize her chances of having a stroke."

We sat silently in the exam room listening to this news. Finally, I said, "So, she might die ... like in a year?" I thought of my mother who had had heart failure a couple of times. Dr. Sametz looked at me, paused, and said, "It is difficult to know." I wasn't ready to lose Cairo.

At home, Cairo took her pills hidden in the Pill Pockets without a fuss. She was alert and didn't show any symptoms of illness besides the rapid breathing. She didn't seem much different than before her diagnosis. She ate less, but her appetite had been waning for years. She still walked around the house and jumped up on to the back of the living room couch to rest from time to time. Despite this, John said, "I think she's uncomfortable because I never see her sleep anymore." I hadn't noticed. I dismissed the vet's warning that she might die soon.

With this new focus on Cairo, I took the time to talk quietly to her and give her belly rubs, something she loved. She had always been unassuming and seemed to appreciate any attention she received. I enjoyed rubbing her tummy and for the first time noticed that it sported a patchwork of orange and black fur amid the white. Even though she had lost some weight, her round face and round belly made her look kitten-like. And the orange triangular patch on her face made her a striking cat.

Two weeks after the visit to the vet, Cairo collapsed while I was out. John heard her coughing and wheezing in the guest bathroom. She struggled and tried to push him away as he picked her up and carried her to the kitchen. John set her down on the kitchen floor where she sank to her side, panting. He timed her breaths at more than sixty per minute.

He instinctively readied Cairo to go to the vet. Despite her weakened state, she resisted as he tried to put her into the cat carrier. He carefully strapped the carrier into the car and drove down the highway as smoothly as possible. Cairo always disliked riding in the car and usually cried constantly. This time she only cried faintly a few times during the twenty-minute ride.

There was not much Dr. Sametz could do. She took Cairo into the procedure room and tried to draw fluid from her lungs, but Cairo fought. The doctor asked John's permission to sedate Cairo, even though it might hasten her death. He agreed. He called me on my cell phone. "Linda, Cairo collapsed today and I'm here with her at the vet. I don't think she'll make it. Dr. Sametz is working on her now, but there isn't too much she can do. Where are you?"

"Oh, John, I'm so sorry. We just started a photo shoot. I will come over as soon as I am done."

John phoned a few minutes later. "Cairo died on the vet's table. I'm going home."

For days, John replayed the scene over and over in his mind. "I shouldn't have taken her to the vet. I knew she was dying. I should have laid her on the bed and just stayed with her until she died."

I thought back to an earlier conversation we had about death. He said he didn't know how anyone could sleep in the bed where someone had died. I wondered wryly if he had envisioned laying Cairo on my side of the bed or his.

I tried to console him. "You were only doing what anyone would do. You were trying to help her. We seek help when a loved one is struggling, even if we know death is near." Nevertheless, his regret remained.

As much as I wished Cairo's last hour had been more serene, the circumstances of her death offered us an opportunity to consider what we wanted when we faced our own deaths. What would be our responsibility to each other: to do everything possible to prolong life or accept the other's decision to die on his or her terms? Cairo's dire situation forced John to make split-second decisions with no time to ponder the implications. He insisted he knew she was dying and should have reacted differently, but I questioned this. He did not have any experience with watching a parent or pet die. I thought he was overly hard on himself. But it was clear to me that we needed to do some thinking and planning for ourselves if we hoped to have control over how we spent our last hours.

I have always wanted to die at home and it seems from John's regret that he valued that, too. Cairo probably would have chosen to be at home, with her family stroking her, as she struggled to breathe in her last hour. Riding in the car and being in the vet's office already evoked terror in her. When death comes, we might as well be comfortable and take the pain relief that medication offers.

When we lived in Massachusetts, Cairo spent many hours on warm summer days sleeping under the broad leaves of the hosta plants in the outdoor cage. That is how we wanted to remember her. After her cremation in North Carolina, I mixed her ashes with the soil of a large potted hosta on our deck. This is where she sleeps now, keeping Steve company, as his ashes feed a nearby potted blue hydrangea, his favorite.

Turning Points

As much as we appreciated Cairo's quiet persona, we found ease in keeping track of only two cats. When we expanded our household by adopting Ebon, I had said to John, "I always wondered why people wanted to have three children. Now I know. Having a third cat makes life so much more interesting."

Years later, after having lived with three cats, I knew why both my mother and I had stopped at two children: Two were much more manageable.

We watched to see what reaction Ebon and Riley had to losing Cairo. They didn't search or sniff or walk aimlessly. Did they notice that she was gone? Do animals just accept a loss and move on? They seemed to be doing just that. They seemed to focus more on each other. Occasionally they acknowledged each other by touching noses. Sometimes Riley sniffed Ebon's neck, then walked closer and, nudging his nose deeper into Ebon's fur, took a nip. This new behavior usually resulted in a squabble.

There were surprising behavior changes. The boys, as I started calling them, seemed to bicker more. Ebon became more aggressive and Riley, in turn, became more defensive. If we followed the sound of a high-pitched growl, we might find Ebon crouched, ears flattened and tail slapping the floor, staring at Riley who took refuge under a dining room chair or the piano bench. Ebon no longer shrank from Riley's stares. His new offensive stance was surprising, but I wonder if he now channeled his natural aggression toward Riley since he no longer had Cairo to harass. Whatever the reason, it seemed as if the playing field had evened.

Ebon had spent a lot of time in our garage, but after asserting himself with Riley, he retreated to the garage less often. In fact, sometimes when he cried at the garage door and we opened it, he stared into the gloom for a few moments, then turned and walked back into the house.

Despite the enmity between Ebon and Riley, the four of us settled into a comfortable routine. Each evening as we watched "The PBS News Hour," followed by "Jeopardy," Riley sat between John and me on the couch. Ebon lounged on the back, inches from our heads, sometimes licking our hair or pawing our scalps. Our adult children lived far away, but we were still a family, cozy and content, with our cats.

In less than a year, our circumstances changed. John was diagnosed with a rare, aggressive bile duct cancer. He seemed to cope with his diagnosis with equanimity and I often heard him humming around the house. At first I found this baffling, but on further thought, I speculated that his humming was similar to a cat's purring to calm itself when sick or in pain. Eventually the multiple rounds of chemotherapy and radiation treatments made John very sick and frayed his nerves. Once a devoted pet parent, he now had little patience for feline shenanigans.

Ebon frequently jumped up on the kitchen counter, even when we were looking right at him. If I was in another room, I could hear John shouting, "Ebon, get down." It never worked. If we stood up to approach him, he jumped off. But John was too tired to stand in response to Ebon's antics. The shouting bothered me, so I bought a yellow water pistol at the local dollar store. We had always had a strict no-guns policy in our home, which included toys, but I was no longer setting an example for children. The necessity of this spray bottle overrode my concern about its shape. Ebon learned quickly that the yellow shape squirted water at him when he was on the counter. Soon, we only had to pick up the toy and Ebon leapt off the counter.

When John received flowers, we put them in the bathroom adjoining our bedroom. We needed to keep them away from Riley who had a penchant for bouquets. If we left the door open, Riley always found the flowers. After he sniffed and tasted them, he invariably knocked over the vases, breaking the ones I valued most. He broke a perfect stoneware cylinder that I had hand-thrown in college and a graceful white Lennox china vase that had been my mother's. Listening to Riley overturn vases and knock toiletries on the floor frustrated John, so we banished Riley from the master bedroom suite.

In the past, the cats curled up next to John in bed when he had a cold, giving him comfort. But things were different with this illness. He felt so sick from the chemotherapy that he did not allow the cats in our bedroom. He wanted no disturbances, no radio, no television, no visitors, and that included his beloved cats. This was a departure from our past roles. Earlier in our marriage, when I found John reading in bed with a cat curled next to him, I had been the one to insist that the cats stay out of our room because of my allergies. Now he was the one banishing the cats. This saddened me because it indicated how ill he felt.

Riley had long enjoyed a nightly routine with John. As John got ready for bed, Riley jumped up on the bathroom counter next to the sink. John turned on the tap so Riley could drink from a thin stream of water. When he finished, Riley sat and watched John for a while, then retreated to the walk-in closet where he perched on a tall dresser. He settled in, probably hoping we would forget he was there. We knew that Riley would wake in the night and keep us from sleeping, so before John got into bed, he escorted Riley out of the closet and directed him through the bedroom door.

After John became ill and did not want Riley in the bedroom, Riley found other places to spend his time. But he was still curious about John. Occasionally I saw him pause at the bedroom door, look in and then continue down the hall. The only time I remember Riley spending time in the bedroom was during John's final days. Our double bed was crowded with John's gel mattress, pillows, a basin, a box of tissues, medical supplies, the electric bed control and John, a thin version of his previous self. Riley curled up inconspicuously on the corner of the bed amidst the paraphernalia. Even when hospice nurses were hovering, I allowed him to stay. John was important to him.

Life was changing. We needed to shift and adjust. I heeded my father's advice and kept busy by nursing John and managing his care. I remembered the lengths to which my parents had gone when my cat Maggie was hit by a car: My father had built a wooden cage to immobilize her and my mother nursed her back to health. They were a team, each using their talents to help Maggie. I had wanted to be a nurse as a child, but gave up the goal when I cut my finger badly and almost fainted. Skill or no skill, I felt compelled to administer John's medicine, change his dressings and take care of his bodily needs. We had always presented ourselves as a team to our children and that hadn't changed.

I wanted to know what he was thinking and feeling, but he didn't share his thoughts readily. I used to say to him during his illness, "If there is something you want to do or someplace you want to go, I will make it happen." And I would have, but he was content to stay at home. Home and family were paramount. I begged to take him for a ride in the countryside to give him a change of scenery. He agreed only when I said he could stay in his pajamas and slippers.

During John's last month of life, we had a busy household with hospice nurses coming a few times a week, equipment deliveries and a constant flow of overnight visitors. Henry came from San Francisco. Close friends sent by our Boston Quaker meeting arrived after that. Grace overlapped their visit and stayed for almost two weeks. John's favorite cousin came from California the night before he died, and John's sister arrived from Minnesota two days later. When the doorbell rang, Riley ran to hide, but Ebon, always curious, ran to the door. We constantly had to keep one leg cocked between the door and the doorframe to make sure Ebon didn't run outside while people were coming in.

Unassuming Cairo had taught us valuable lessons. She entered our home a fearful, skittish cat, but John's patience and gentleness won her over. Love is powerful. She remained quiet and undemanding, but she was the one who had told me Steve was sick. When she died, she taught us a lesson that became critical sooner than we expected. John regretted taking Cairo to the vet when he felt she was dying. She didn't want to be picked up, put in her carrier, ride in the car or go to the vet. She wanted to lie down and breathe easily. John wished he had laid her on the bed and stayed with her until she died.

Six months after John's diagnosis, his doctor said, "I think you should enter hospice care." We were stunned. John gasped and sobbed. After the initial shock of hearing these words, John said, "I know what I want to do. I want to die at home."

If there can be a good death, John had one. In the months before his death, he cleaned out and organized all his personal papers. Together we sorted everything in the house, especially the boxes filled with mysterious plumbing and electrical supplies in the garage, things I knew I would never use. We listed for sale a major power tool from his woodshop. We had time to say important things to each other. He did not linger in pain for too many months. When he died, he was surrounded by people who loved him.

Immediately after John's death, I pictured the cats searching frantically for him or moping around because of his absence, but I saw none of this behavior. They had responded so positively to the years of his regular schedule, his predictability, that I was sure they would feel the loss. Maybe they knew what was happening as they sat in his room in those last days.

Whatever they felt or took in, it was clear that they now knew I was the only one to feed them or to offer company in the evening. As I sat at my desk filling out forms, reviewing legal documents and shuffling bank accounts, both cats wanted to be close: so close that they lay down on the papers next to my computer as I tended to my deskwork. I finally put two cat baskets on either side of my monitor to get them off the papers. It didn't work. We continued to jockey for position so I could get work done. I loved having them close and I didn't put them out of the room.

At twelve, Riley had slowed down and become more vulnerable. He used to stare adoringly at John and stay close to his side. Now he had lost his ally. John's death offered Ebon a chance to assume dominance. A naturally confident cat, he had weathered Riley's abuse for years. Riley had been in control because he had lived in our home before Ebon, but Ebon had the natural temperament for dominance.

Ebon became more aggressive after Cairo's death and he stepped up this behavior a month after John's death. Ebon harassed Riley three or four times a day and Riley spent more time hiding under chairs and tables. The dominant cat in the household had shifted. One change in the family had cascaded to another.

◆ ◆ ◆

Fortunately, our grown children's behavior was not as dramatic as the cats' reaction to John's death. Grace and Henry responded in keeping with their personalities. Grace visited John every month while he was ill and cried at times; Henry kept his feelings to himself but flew in from his job in Bulgaria for his father's memorial service. In many families after a parent's death, the siblings become estranged. In our case, Henry and Grace seemed to enjoy each other's company more.

FLYING SOLO

On My Own

After John died, I stayed in our house. I had pushed our furniture around for years and had finally settled on an arrangement I liked. I didn't want to start over. The house was perfect for the cats: It was split into two territories, possessed a screened porch and had a long hallway where Ebon ran when he needed to stretch his legs.

Once again, I followed my father's advice and kept myself busy with volunteer work, choral rehearsals, aqua aerobics classes, doctor appointments, lunches with friends and bereavement groups. Just as I had cleaned out my parents' clothing within days of their deaths, I had John's clothing picked up by a local charity right away. I swept away his presence so I didn't have to face my loss and feel the pain. I remained in denial for nine months. I was full of hope for the future and surprisingly cheerful.

My relationship with Riley and Ebon changed. We were three now. When I was home, they wanted to be with me. If they weren't with me I wanted the reassurance of knowing where they were. They kept me company in the family room as I watched television. I had never liked having a cat on my lap, but now I found it comforting for ten or fifteen minutes. Often Ebon crawled onto my chest with his face close to mine. I stroked and petted him, and tried to avoid his bad breath. I told him, "I know where that mouth has been." Riley liked to knead my body, just as he had done with John.

When I went to my home office to use the computer or write checks, both cats accompanied me. Ebon wanted to be close, very close. When he draped himself over my open laptop, I pushed him away. He sat up and moved so close to my hands and face that I needed to lean away. It seemed as if he constantly wanted to be stroked or kissed. If I got up to go to the bathroom, he came with me and rubbed against my legs as I sat on the toilet.

Cat care had to change after John died. With my busy schedule, I didn't have time to drive home every day to feed Ebon lunch or even dinner on some days. Over the years, John had increased feeding the cats from two to four meals a day. They started out with breakfast and dinner, but then John added a snack before bed. After he retired, he gave them lunch, too, especially when Ebon begged. John, an old softy, would say, "OK, Ebon, just a little food," as he poured a small amount of kibble into Ebon's dish for lunch. I fed them two full meals and a snack at night. Ebon exhibited good manners by sitting patiently on the floor as I chopped his wet cat food into bite-sized pieces. Riley jumped onto the counter and stuck his nose into the cat food can, even though he wouldn't have eaten it if I had given it to him. He was a picky eater and was in his dry food phase. His palate would change unexpectedly so I was never sure what he would eat.

To accommodate my schedule, I bought an automatic feeder with a timer. I loaded it with dry food, set the timer to open at dinnertime, and put it on Ebon's placemat on the floor when I was not going to be home. When I returned, the automatic dish was always empty. One day I noticed that the dish was out of its automatic base, as if Ebon had forced it open. I soon realized that Ebon pried open the dish as soon as I left the house.

I tried to keep the food away from him until I left for the day. One morning before leaving I carried the automatic feeder around with me and set it down on the hall table to answer the phone. Ebon found the feeder and knocked it off the table. It popped open and cat kibble scattered all over the hall floor. Reluctant to brush it into a dustpan and mix it with dust, I left it for him to eat, piece by piece. As I had hoped, when I returned home that evening, the floor was clean. I also found I could leave dishes in the sink and Ebon would lick them clean by the time I returned. I didn't even need to rinse them before I put them into the dishwasher.

John had indulged Riley by turning on the bathroom faucet so Riley could drink from a thin stream of water. I continued this practice until I realized I frequently forgot to shut off the tap when I left the room. I purchased a cat fountain and installed it at one end of the kitchen counter. The fountain was a big hit.

With only one adult in the house to police the kitchen, the cats roamed the counters whenever they pleased. I used to have Riley trained to stay on the lowered desk at the end of the counter where the water fountain sat, but his fascination with water led him across the counter to the sink. He crouched there as I prepared dinner or washed dishes. I allowed this, rationalizing that this was a stimulating hobby for him. He extended his territory to the counter on the other side of the sink, too, but always hurried off when he saw me coming.

Ebon trolled the counters every time he thought I wasn't looking, even when I sat a few feet away. If I left freshly baked muffins to cool, I found muffins with bites out of them. If I hid muffins in the microwave, I found the microwave moved away from the wall. When I left frozen shrink-wrapped chicken on the counter to thaw, I found it several feet away in the sink. I left a hard-cooked egg on the counter while I stepped out of the kitchen one morning and found it under the couch when I returned. No amount of shouting motivated him to get off the counter. He jumped down only when I walked toward him, as if he was afraid I would hit him. We never did.

Just as Ebon made his move to dominate Riley, he started to push boundaries with me, too. I still fed Riley on demand since he ate small amounts and always left some in the dish. I put his dish in the cupboard where it sat on top of a plastic container a few inches from the shelf above. Ebon always checked to see if I had remembered to put the childproof lock on the cat food cupboard. If not, he opened the door, stood on his hind legs and ate any of Riley's leftover kibble. He had to turn his head sideways to eat the food. Each time I left the door unlocked I found an empty food bowl in the cupboard.

I washed the cats' dishes—durable white melamine with nonskid rubber on the bottom—each time they ate out of them. Occasionally, I didn't have a clean one and put Riley's kibble into a glass dessert bowl. The day Ebon discovered this bowl in the cupboard, he also discovered that he could move it. With a sweep of his paw, the dish tumbled out of the cupboard and smashed on the granite countertop. Kibble and glass shards were on the counter, the floor, the windowsill and in the sink. I had to carry Ebon out of the vicinity to make sure he didn't eat any of the glass as he gobbled up the kibble.

Ebon was still the same spunky cat we adopted ten years earlier, but he had mellowed. He rarely played with cat toys anymore. After each meal, he sat in front of the garage door waiting to go out. If I didn't notice him in five or ten minutes, he cried. I made a sign that said, "Cat in Garage." When he went out there, I hung it on the door. I feared getting into the car and driving off, forgetting he was in the garage. Once I drove part of the way up my driveway and saw a black cat in my yard. "Oh, that looks like Ebon," I mused. "Yikes! That *is* Ebon!" When the garage door went up, he walked out.

Riley had changed a lot in twelve years. He went from being an aggressive cat that attacked us most days to being a sweet, cooperative cat that liked to stay close. Prozac had a lot to do with that change. I still wiped transdermal Prozac cream on the inside of his ear, but he hid every night when he saw me get the medicine from the cupboard. Nothing about this procedure hurt him, but perhaps he didn't like having his ears touched.

Riley vocalized more than he did as a young cat. When he entered my office, he would walk up to my desk and give me a loud meow. At first, I thought he wanted food, but when I followed him to the kitchen, he refused the food. It seemed as if he wanted me in the kitchen instead of my office.

He had an opinion about my singing at the piano, too. Now that I was no longer singing soprano, and developing my lower voice, he didn't seem to like it. He stared at me as I sang. If I didn't stop, he jumped up on the piano bench, meowing. I thought he wanted to sing along until the day he pawed and bit me. It may have been the pitch. I have heard that cats like higher pitched voices.

◆ ◆ ◆

The first year after John died, I took five trips. In the fall, I held one of his memorial services in North Carolina, the other in Boston. Grace attended both and Henry flew in from Bulgaria to attend the one in Boston. For Thanksgiving, I wanted to be by myself and visited museums in Washington, D.C. At Christmas, I met my children and my son's boyfriend in San Diego. In June, I rented a beach house with my daughter and her boyfriend. In July, Henry, Grace and I met John's cousin and her daughter in California for the anniversary of John's death. I was full of energy and optimistic about my future: I was clearly in denial.

A boyfriend from forty-five years ago visited in the spring after John's death. He was surprised by my upbeat attitude and started to refer to me as Pollyanna. When he left after the weekend, I relived the loss of both John and him. I wept every day for the next two months.

As I grew closer to my children, I also grew closer to my cats. When I traveled, I left Ebon and Riley in the hands of a devoted cat sitter who visited them twice a day. When one trip took me away for nine days, I felt guilty and invited a neighbor to read in my house to keep the cats company. I missed them more and more each time I traveled.

Pushing the Envelope

The second year after John's death I took four trips. I went back to Boston in August, again at Thanksgiving, spent Christmas in Buenos Aires with Henry and Grace and went on a Caribbean cruise. I returned to Boston for three months the following summer, but took Ebon and Riley with me. I couldn't be away from them for that long. I put down a deposit on a furnished one-bedroom apartment in November and spent the next six months thinking about the logistics of getting two cats to Boston. Ebon had been getting increasingly aggressive with Riley so I asked the vet to put him on Prozac. With both cats on Prozac, life in a small apartment might work out.

Ebon still suffered from motion sickness. I had experimented giving him motion sickness medication, but he still vomited before I could drive out of my neighborhood. Grace agreed to fly from Boston to Raleigh, pick up Ebon and fly back to Boston the same day. She stayed with him in my rented apartment until I drove to Boston with Riley. With the vet's permission, I gave Ebon a double dose of anti-nausea medicine and drove him to the airport. As I turned off the exit and entered the maze of airport arteries I heard a ticking sound. With dread I muttered, "Oh no, not a car problem the day before I drive to Boston." As I listened I realized it was Ebon panting.

I parked in the airport garage and waited for him to stabilize. He was foaming at the mouth. He declined all offers of food, water and treats. Tired of waiting for us in the airport, Grace joined us in the car. "The car stinks, Mom," she said as she got into the back seat. However, Ebon had not thrown up or peed in the carrier. The car did smell, but I hadn't noticed.

When Ebon calmed down, we went into the terminal and the three of us sat at a table in a sandwich shop. I opened Ebon's carrier and put it on one of the chairs. He sat up at the table with a paper plate in front of him as he ate bits of cheese from Grace's pizza. Although he was leashed, I kept my hand on his shoulders to make sure he did not jump out of his carrier.

Ebon had his own luggage. I had imagined all the scenarios my daughter might encounter and packed accordingly. His suitcase contained a litter box and large bag of litter; two gift box tops to be used as disposable litter boxes in the ladies' room at the airport with two small bags of litter; a scratching box; six cans of cat food; a small bag of kibble; a bag of treats; toys and catnip bubbles; a sheet with Ebon's scent on it to make him feel at home in the new apartment; bottles of cat pheromones and a plug-in dispenser to calm him; his new prescription of Prozac; his dish and water bowl; extra towels for his carrier in case of motion sickness; instructions on how much to feed him; and an admonition not to yell at or raise a hand to him. In addition to the cat in a carrier, my daughter had to contend with his rolling suitcase.

I had spent months worrying that travel might endanger the cats. Ebon could escape during a TSA check or bathroom break at the airport; Riley might get free of his halter at a highway rest stop or escape from a hotel room while I was at dinner. The idea of losing one of them was too much to bear. The stress of travel and apartment living might be too much for their aging souls.

Grace reported that Ebon was fine on the flight and in her car, but I still worried about him as I drove from North Carolina to Boston. The trip took four days because I visited friends along the way. It was a stressful trip for me with no one to help navigate the highways or keep me company. Each day brought a new battle with my GPS as it defaulted to a main highway after I had specified an alternate route. I took many wrong turns and had to figure out how to get back on track by sneaking peeks at Google maps on my iPad or by pushing buttons on the car's navigation system. I missed exits because of heavy traffic and lost time backtracking to find a pet friendly hotel for Riley.

Everything seemed to take longer with no one to help me drag all our gear into a friend's home or a motel. Riley handled the strangeness by hiding under the beds at all of our overnight stays. When we arrived in Boston, Riley hid under the bed there, too, for a week. Grace had set up the apartment nicely and Ebon seemed content.

I was proud that the cats adjusted as well as they did. However, I was sure they would rather have been at home sitting on their screened porch watching deer and squirrels in the yard, not sitting on a windowsill watching cars in the parking lot. If they weren't in the window or sleeping, they sat by the apartment door, hoping to escape into the hall. I walked them on their leashes in the building, up and down stairs as they explored the scents on the carpet or the various welcome mats as we walked past door after door. They learned not to flinch when they heard the high-pitched yap of the small dog across the hall. They found places to sleep in the apartment: comfortable couches and carpeted floors, all things that hold dust and cat dander and irritate my sinuses. I took time to play with them and was diligent about not leaving them alone for too long.

On the second anniversary of John's death, Grace and I had dinner at a restaurant on the Boston harbor. I had a fond memory of this place because John and I had eaten here years ago. Grace asked, "Do you still think about Dad a lot?" I replied, "I try not to. It makes me too sad. It doesn't do any good to wallow in my sadness. I need to move forward." I thought later that I had learned my parents' lessons well: Keep moving; don't dwell on what's lost.

The Boston trip was part of the journey of finding my solo self after thirty-six years of happy marriage. John and I raised our children and started our cat adventure in Boston. Our family had morphed and our children had grown into adults. Cats had come and gone.

I have learned a lot from my cats. With every change in their lives, they quietly adjust. When John died, they didn't plan, they didn't keep busy, they just accepted the change and continued living their lives. When they found themselves in a strange apartment in Boston, they found new places to sleep, new windowsills to sit on, new things to observe. I would do well to emulate them. They are great life and traveling partners, as are my children. Our household has changed, but we have all adapted.

Now, at home, it is nice to know that the cats and I can adjust and find new paths together. We are a team, a family, and we will stick together. We always have.

Acknowledgements

Thank you to Ruth Harriet Jacobs who encouraged me to write my first cat story.

Joyce Allen's writing group was a tremendous support in the creation of this book. I produced story after story about my cats and they listened to them again and again as I made refinements over the years. They asked good questions and pushed for more details. Thank you Joyce Allen, Barbara Brister, Karan Freimark, Janice Gebel, Linda Kampel, Andrea Savage, Anne Tasewell and John Wurzelmann.

My beta readers, Faye Ashley, Carolyn Cooper, Cathy Dobbins, Margaret Kane, Tad McArdle and Naomi Mendelsohn, were invaluable as I gauged their reactions and made adjustments to the story line.

Thanks, too, to Mike McArdle for suggesting the book title after hearing one of the more trying stories at a dinner party.

Nora Gaskin Esthimer and Dawn Reno Langley pushed me to dive deeper for which I will be forever grateful. Nora also provided the structure and detail orientation needed to lead me smoothly through the book production process. Thank you.

Thank you to Karen N.V. Owen who provided detailed, consistent and well-researched editing.

I enjoyed working with Beth Tashery Shannon, the Frogtown Bookmaker, and appreciate her willingness to collaborate with an opinionated former graphic designer (me).

I am very grateful I knew published authors Joyce Allen, Carol Henderson and Ruth Moose who were generous with their time and read my finished manuscript. And, very grateful that the veterinarians at Jordan Lake Animal Hospital, Leslie Staggs and Holly Weston, took the time to read the book and comment.

My son, Henry Andrew Watterson, was generous with his time and read the manuscript in its very early stage and later close to completion. The early draft came back covered in red ink; the later one had only a few typed comments. I thank both of my children, but particularly my daughter, Grace Watterson, for giving me permission to include some of the more private aspects of our lives.

Finally, thank you to all the cats that entrusted their lives to our care.

Biography

Linda Patterson grew up with cats, but developed an allergy to them by the time she was a teenager. Despite this, she brought cats back into her life after her marriage to a cat lover. These later experiences inspired her to write this book.

As a small child, she and her brother were encouraged to tell stories at the dinner table. She continued telling stories graphically for thirty years as a designer and then in direct marketing where she fell in love with writing. Years later she combined her visual talents, verbal story telling and writing skill by producing stories for a public television magazine show.

She resides in North Carolina with her two cats, Ebon and Riley.

www.ingramcontent.com/pod-product-compliance
Lightning Source LLC
Chambersburg PA
CBHW030437010526
44118CB00011B/677